The Unbeatable Man

Matt Furey

The Unbeatable Man

Matt Furey

ISBN Softbound: 978-0-9819320-3-3
ISBN Hardbound: 978-0-9819320-5-7

Published in the United States of America by:
　　Gold Medal Publications, Inc.
　　10339 Birdwatch Drive
　　Tampa, Florida 33647
　　Tel: (813) 994-8267 * FAX (813) 994-4947
　　Email: matt@mattfurey.com Website: mattfurey.com

Layout and Design by Vincent Lai

Dedication

To Frank, Faith and Zhannie

Based on a true story.

Names and other details fictionalized
at the author's discretion.

One

I grew up in a small town in Iowa that called itself a "city." 10,000 of us were surrounded by acres of farms with seven-foot corn stalks and mile-long rows of bean fields. Each day when I stepped outside my house and looked north I was greeted by a greenish-blue water tower hovering a hundred feet above me. The city's name, CARROLL, shown across its dome in black paint.

My house was only a hundred fifty feet from this water tower but my home was located several miles away. My home was in the wrestling room at my high school. This home was filled with red and gold mats, with barbells and dumbbells and weight machines. My home had a locker room where I stored training gear, it had showers for me to wash the salty sweat from my body after practice; it had a scale for me to keep track of the pounds I needed to drop before a match and it had an empty space on the wall where I imagined my name and my accomplishments would be painted someday. This empty space would say: Matt Furey – State Champion.

More than any other place, I was comfortable in a wrestling room; comfortable in the midst of brawling men whose frames were shredded with muscle. The first time I journeyed into this home and stepped onto those red and gold mats I felt a chill; a chill of excitement in a room where the temperature was never less than 80 degrees.

The heat promoted mental toughness and helped with weight loss. As I learned to push, pummel and pry against the limbs of my teammates, as I learned to move my body into and around the force of another, my t-shirt and shorts were sopped in sweat.

The sport of wrestling, more than any other, captured my spirit. It puzzled me with its complexity and wooed me with its passion. There were so many moves, set-ups and combinations; so many counters to any maneuver ever attempted, so many different styles of combat – there was so much to learn and I was intrigued by it all because the learning never stopped.

I fell in love with a sport that was damn near impossible to master. Mastery required the ability to execute holds while countering an opponent's. Mastery required strategy, a focused mind, and the ability to negotiate for position with any opponent, regardless of his size, shape, speed or strength. Mastery required automatic reflexes. And it required time, commitment and a ton of unquenchable desire.

Loren Greenfield was my high school coach and early on during my freshman year, he told me, "Matt, when you know these moves well enough to do them in your sleep, without thinking, you're on the road to mastery." Boy, was he ever right.

Wrestling taught me self-control, discipline and pride. It gave me a purpose in life. It gave me faith in the future. It was in wrestling rooms and on wrestling mats that I directed my life and planned my future; it was where I gained peace of mind, even if only for a while.

At the age of 14, after winning an all-freshman wrestling tournament; a tournament filled with kids from "big city schools" (as my dad liked to call them), I made a decision to be the best wrestler in the state, in my weight class, by the time I was a senior.

After I made that decision I trained like a madman. I did calisthenics, lifted weights, ran distance, pounded up hills, drilled wrestling techniques, jumped rope and sat up at night reading wrestling books and biographies of other great athletes.

My favorite book was about my idol, Dan Gable, the 1972 Olympic gold medalist at 149.5 pounds and the head wrestling coach at the University of Iowa. He was the man I patterned my life after. He was the man I wanted to be coached by someday.

During the summer I enrolled in camps where I would meet and learn from Gable. And it was at his camps that I devoured the best techniques available from him as well as other collegiate, world and Olympic champions; people with names like Robinson, Campbell and Yagla; people named Banach and Lewis; people called Zalesky, Davis, DeAnna and Trizzino. I wanted to be like all of these men and I believed that if I worked hard enough toward my desire – someday my efforts would pay off.

During my first three years of high school many people laughed at my desire and my unusual discipline. Some called me "muscle head," "macho man" and "dumb jock." Some laughed about my chosen sport, saying "only queers roll around on a mat with other men." These people thought I took sports and life too seriously. But I was doing what I set out to do. I was living my dream. And part of that dream came to life in the winter of 1981, when I went to Des Moines to compete in the Iowa High School State Wrestling Championships.

Long before I went to Des Moines I knew I had something to prove to the people who laughed at me. I had something to prove to those people who told me, "Furey, you'll never, ever qualify for the state meet." I would do more than qualify. I would come home the champ. Other than wrestling for Gable, that was my number one desire.

My earliest wrestling experiences began in the living room of the house I lived in. My parents had seven children: six boys and a girl. I was the fifth of six boys and the sixth child, arriving after my sister, Sheila. Two of my older brothers spent their spare time beating the hell out of me. So part of my desire to wrestle and become great was not only the challenge of the sport; it was the exodus I thought it gave me, a pathway through the limitations I felt imprisoned by.

When I was 13 my determination to escape from my family's shackles hit its peak when an older brother almost killed me. I always felt like he would have liked to kill me and I'm lucky he never did. On this occasion he whooped me so hard in the head, that I not only saw stars, I thought I was entering the tunnel that begins the after-life process. Lucky for me, another older brother ran to the basement where the violence was erupting, and stopped him in his tracks. The two began fighting and although one was much shorter and smaller than the other, he found a way to even the score by tossing a half-full can of white paint at his head. The paint can barely missed the bigger brother's head as it opened, then splattered against the wall and stairs, giving our black Labrador, Jake, a new coat for his ears.

When I regained enough consciousness to return to my feet, I vowed to be the toughest boy in the family. "IN TWO YEARS," I screamed, loud enough for every family member to hear, "I'M GOING TO BEAT THE LIVING SHIT OUT OF YOU. YOU WON'T DARE LAY ANOTHER HAND ON ME AGAIN."

The bench mark I set for myself started to unfold one afternoon when I was

16. It was during the hot, humid month of July, and this same brother, who almost killed me, was dropping me off at home, after a day out detasseling corn. As I opened the door to the car he called me a dickhead in front of his college buddy, and my retort, which was instantaneous, was to call him an asshole.

He hated the inference and chased after me. I started to run for the front door, trying to outrace him, but half way there, I thought, "Kick his ass. Here's the chance you've been waiting for. You're a lot tougher than he is now. Beat the shit out of this creep."

I turned around and locked him up in a bear hug and threw his ass on the grass. My fists were moving toward his pearly whites when his buddy grabbed me and began pulling me off. My mom was screaming for us to stop while our dog Jake was biting into my brother's leg. The fight ended almost as quickly as it started and he never touched me again. Afterward, as so often happens, the very people you slug it out with become your friends and allies.

Besides my vow to be tougher than my older brothers, I made other vows. Secret vows.

One, I would not hang around anyone who was not the type of person I wanted to become.

Two, I would study, practice and do whatever it took to become great.

Three, I would not touch drugs; I would not drink. I would not do anything that could jeopardize my career or prevent me from becoming a champion.

The path I chose was not an easy one. It required physical and mental discipline I hadn't developed yet. It required me to listen to anyone whom I thought could help me become a better athlete. And that's precisely why the wrestling room became my home.

It was there that I found coaches who would inspire me, who would encourage me.

* * * * *

As I lived up to the vows I set for myself, I encountered many challenges. One time, when I was a sophomore, I went to a beer party with my friend, John, a 6' 4" would-be animal who wrestled heavyweight and played tackle on the football team. At this party a short stocky farmer named Dan came up to me, flanked with a group of his buddies. He tried to pick a fight with me by poking his finger into my chest and repeatedly telling me I was a loser, a nothing, a nobody. As he took a gulp from his beer glass he asked me why I didn't drink, then he threw the rest of his beer on me while his friends stood around and laughed.

I don't know how I was able to keep calm, to silently take the abuse. It was probably because I recognized that anything I did could have resulted in my getting pummeled by twenty of his friends, most of whom were as drunk as he was and didn't like me much either. But maybe it was my way of seeing if I could block what was happening out of my mind.

When I was in third grade and was easily irritated by other students in class, my mother told me, "Matt, if you think you can't concentrate in class because of the other students, just imagine there is a wall between you and them. Imagine that this wall blocks them out of your mind. If you do this, I'm sure you won't have any trouble concentrating."

I used the technique in third grade and it worked like magic. After a few weeks it quickly became a habit, and so I was unconsciously using it at the beer party that night. No matter how hard Dan tried to get a violent reaction from me, he couldn't. He dished out at least fifteen minutes of insults and I let all of it float off into space. Yet, deep inside I used everything he was saying as fuel to drive me onward and upward. I would eventually show him who the real loser was – all I needed was more time to train and prepare myself.

As I left the party that night I made more silent vows to myself. First, I would never go to another high school beer party again. Second, I would show everyone at that party that they were wrong about me. I was going to be a winner. Their insults were going to be catalysts that increased my desire to succeed. No one was going to hold me down. I would rise above all of them.

But my method of rising above them would not be done via fist fights at beer parties. It wouldn't be done in shouting matches or arguments. It would be done on wrestling mats – in high schools gyms and auditoriums throughout the state. In conquering the best any school in the state had, I would, without saying a word or lifting a fist, simultaneously defeat the mockers and the jeerers, those who weren't man enough to dedicate themselves to a goal, to focus on it, to do what it takes to succeed while eliminating any negative habit that could prevent success.

The list of people I had something to prove to kept growing; it became so enormous that my perception of how I stacked up with others became the most dominant thought in my mind. I was either going to rise above them all or fall victim to a life of mediocrity. The right choice was obvious, I thought. The world gives no awards to critics. Awards are given to those who don't care what the others think; those who pursue their passion and succeed in spite of detractors.

And so, as I traveled past the fields and farms on the way to Des Moines, where I would display my talents before the greatest wrestling fans in the country, I had something to prove to myself and to everyone who doubted me. Yet, inside of me, intertwined with my intense desire to rise up and become a champion, I was really nothing more than a "regular" guy who wanted what everyone else wants in life: respect, love, appreciation and the feeling of being important.

Winning wrestling matches was my path to freedom. Wrestling was my path to self-respect.

The path wasn't easy. But it was the path I chose and it brought purpose and meaning into my life.

These are the memories of my youth, and these memories will never leave me. They are indelibly etched into my mind; they are chiseled onto my body. They run with me today when I pull the hood up on my sweatshirt and stride down the road of life. They sit with me when I rest at the end of each day. They scroll through my mind when I sleep at night.

And within the vast arena of my mind, where crowds have gathered to see me compete; where awards are given to conquerors; where newspaper reporters and television crews gather to record high school wrestling history; THAT is where my memories take shape and come into focus.

Let me tell you about them.

Let me tell you ALL about them.

Two

On a cold, chilly Wednesday afternoon in February of 1981, Coach Greenfield and I arrived in Des Moines for the state wrestling tournament that I, for the first time, would be competing in. I remember sitting in the locker room of Veteran's Memorial Auditorium, waiting for the referee to call the 167-pound class up to the scales for weigh-ins. That year, I didn't have a problem with my weight, usually being a few pounds light. So you never saw me running around in plastic sweats, jumping rope, doing calisthenics, or expending energy to drop several pounds of water weight. But Wayne Love was.

Wayne Love was the defending state champion in my weight class. He was tall and muscular, built like a Greek god. When I saw him walking around before weigh-ins, I couldn't believe he and I were in the same weight class. His biceps and forearms were HUGE. He had muscles upon muscles, some that I didn't think existed. His thighs were long, like a bull moose, but thick and powerful like a rhinoceros.

Love looked like he could rip your arms and legs from your body at the speed of sound. Man, I was scared when I looked at him. And I don't mind saying so.

Contributing to my fear was the fact that Love hadn't tasted defeat in over two years. Love was more than last year's returning champion – he was the best wrestler of the tournament and one of the greatest athletes to ever come out of the state of Iowa. He was good – damn good – and everyone knew it – even I knew it. I was good, too, but hardly anyone knew this, including me, much of the time.

What I did know, though, was what I heard Coach Greenfield saying to the team for years. Coach Greenfield wore a thick black beard during the season and when he talked to the team you could see traces of his days as a collegiate wrestler etched onto his face. He hobbled and limped whenever the weather was cold, his knees still aching from injuries suffered long ago. He wore wire rim glasses that he took on and off whenever he demonstrated techniques, and whenever he spoke to us after practice his intentions were clear: he wanted to motivate us. To do so he would cup his hands to each side of his mouth, as if he were yelling across a football field. Then, oddly, he'd talk to us in a normal voice.

"Listen up everyone. We're a week away from the district tournament. This is the tournament that qualifies you for the state meet next weekend, provided you place first or second. So realize that you have a chance to make it to state. A lot of guys at the district meet are tired of wrestling. They would rather have the season over and done with. They're tired of cutting weight. They're tired of dieting. They're tired of practicing every night after school. So you've got a chance against these guys, even if you think they're better than you."

"So remember what the big key to winning is: It's taking one match at a time; looking ahead only in the sense of knowing what your overall goal for the tournament is, but keeping your feet on the ground by realizing you have to win one match at a time to get to the finals."

"The worst thing you can do is assume you're in the finals or that you've got the tournament won, when you haven't wrestled your first match yet."

Most of my teammates didn't have the desire or the discipline to become great, they didn't see themselves as having a chance to qualify for state, so the truth is I was one of a handful on the team who cared about his message. Yes, it was sad to see so many of my teammates looking as eager to finish their season as the hypothetical athletes Coach Greenfield spoke about. But I couldn't change them. I could only look after myself. So I made damn sure my mind was totally focused on extending my season as long as possible. Truth is I never wanted it to end. So I absorbed Coach Greenfield's words and to prove it, before each tournament began I put his message into an abbreviated format. When I mentally prepared for each match I would repeat to myself, like a mantra, the following: *One match at a time. One match at a time.*

This mantra was especially important in Des Moines because in less than 24 hours I would be squaring off in my first-round match. If I won, I would be in the quarterfinals against the state champion, Wayne Love, whom everyone in the state, including the coaches from all the top colleges, would be watching. All eyes would be upon him.

And almost no one would be watching for this guy named Matt Furey, from a Catholic high school called Kuemper. He was an unranked nobody from a school that rarely had wrestlers represent the school at the state meet. Only one ever won the state title, Dick Conley, in 1963. And before this tournament began, only two others had even qualified for the state meet. I was the fourth to be in the tournament at all.

* * * * *

During the spring of my junior year, Mark Dalton, the head football coach, pulled me aside during gym class and said, "Matt, a lot of kids go out for sports at Kuemper, but only a few of them have really dedicated themselves to sports like you have. You keep working like you have and you're destined to become great."

The difference between me and the rest of the athletes Coach Dalton was talking about was evident in the 0-9 record the football team had when I was a junior. I was on the team that year and because I felt like I was wasting time better spent on wrestling, I made a painful decision that was difficult to relay to Coach Dalton. But it had to be done – and my timing couldn't have been worse. Right after receiving these words of praise, I told him that I wouldn't be on the football team my senior year.

He didn't like hearing me say this, so he nodded his head as if he agreed, then asked, "Do you want to graduate?"

"Of course I want to graduate," I said.

"Well, how do you expect to graduate if you don't pass phys ed? I'm the P.E. teacher you know, and I'll flunk you if you don't play football."

"You wouldn't flunk me in P.E. just because I concentrated on wrestling," I said, trying to see if he was serious.

He paused a minute, making me squirm a bit, then laughed and said, "I'm sure you're making the right decision. I support you all the way. Good luck."

Coach Dalton knew that far too many kids from my school who could have been great never would be because they were more into partying, being accepted, and being part of the crowd. He knew I stood alone and pursued what really mattered to me. As much as he wanted me on his football team he also knew what mattered the most to me was being a great wrestler. He knew I wanted to win the state title and attend college on a scholarship. Having his support meant a lot, but if necessary, I was prepared to go without it.

Three

In the middle of Veteran's Memorial Auditorium on Thursday afternoon, after hours, weeks, months and years of hard work, I was in the arena where I would get the respect I desired. The wrestling arena. Day one of the tournament was underway and with the excitement of a restless child, I waited for my turn on the mat.

As I stood in the warm-up area loosening my limbs, waiting for my name to be called, I knew that in a few minutes I would be competing before 15,000 people; 5000 more people than the population of my hometown. I kept looking upward, clasping and re-clasping my hands, trying to keep a hold of myself, physically and mentally. Like an automaton I followed a series of superstitious warm-up habits.

When the matches in my weight class began to be called, I took off my sweat top. Slowly, I pulled the zipper down, methodically removed my right arm, then my left. I gently folded the red and gold sleeves, making certain they were perfectly creased. My sweat pants came off next. Still moving slowly, I pulled the material over my right wrestling shoe, then the left. In a prayer-like manner, I treated my warm-ups like they were sacred, as if how they were folded somehow controlled the result of my upcoming match. Neat and tidy signified a flawless match. Sloppy and slovenly represented an embarrassing, ignominious defeat.

From the time I was a freshman I followed this eccentric behavior. I blocked out of my mind the times my sweats were meticulously folded and placed in a safe spot, where no one could disturb them, and I still endured a crushing, bruising defeat. Yet, I didn't think about questioning why I had so many superstitious quirks. After all, doing so might cause a defeat, too.

The longer I waited for my bout to be called, the more excited I became. I couldn't wait to hear my name announced. In my mind, in the confusing commotion of the crowd, it seemed like I had already heard my name called a thousand times. When my nervousness became unbearable, I gazed heavenward, and upon seeing the roof of the auditorium I prayed as if God was looking right at me, observing my every thought and move. He was not only listening to me, but was giving me the power to fulfill my dreams.

God, give me the strength to perform to the best of my ability. Keep me free from injury. Help me to win. Help me become somebody. Give me the strength to go home a state champion.

When I finished my prayer, the announcer's voice sounded like thunder cracking through the sky in a summer rain storm. "167 POUNDS. ON DECK MAT FIVE. MATT FUREY OF CARROLL KUEMPER VERSUS TERRY HAMMES OF FAIRFIELD. FUREY VERSUS HAMMES, ON DECK MAT FIVE. PLEASE REPORT."

My chest expanded as I took a deep breath. Adrenaline shot through my veins. I looked at my coach. Simultaneously, we started running for the mat I'd be competing on. Once I arrived at Mat 5, I jumped up and down to loosen my body even more, removing every last trace of tension.

I was in a trance. I ignored the crowds, I ignored the other matches, I ignored the details noticed only by spectators.

Everything around me was in slow motion. I felt like I was moving within a dream – yet it didn't seem like a dream. This was the most real life had ever felt to me. A funny feeling, almost like I had no control – but was totally in control at the same time. What a moment. I trained for four years to enter this match, yet the feelings I was experiencing were something I could not rehearse. I could not experience them before they happened. What controlled these feelings seemed to come from beyond my own consciousness.

The match before me sped by. 10 seconds showed on the clock. I took off my gold t-shirt with Kuemper Wrestling silk-screened on the front, and pulled the straps on my singlet up, then silently counted along with the clock, "10, 9, 8..."

When I walked onto the soft 42' x 42' mat I told myself that I had to win, that this was IT, that there was no turning back. I shifted all gears into overdrive – the only gear I wanted to be in.

My opponent, Terry Hammes, was tall and lanky with obvious tendon strength in his forearms that would give him added leverage. Me, I was short and stocky with bulging triceps and thick, muscular thighs. My body knew hard-core training, it was accustomed to it, and whenever I looked bigger and stronger than an opponent I felt a surge of confidence.

I can whip this guy. I'm bigger and stronger than he is.

Of course I didn't have the muscle mass of Wayne Love, but if I lost to Hammes I'd never wrestle him anyway, so I put Love out of my mind for the moment and focused on the only match that counted.

After we shook hands the referee blew his whistle to begin the bout. I thought I would have an easy time beating Hammes, but I was in for a surprise. The long, lanky guy attacked me with a low-level single leg, trapping me below the knee. The leverage of his arms was insurmountable and he hoisted my leg up toward the sky and tripped my planted foot out from under me. The clock had only clicked off 10 seconds and I was on the ground. "Two-point takedown, green," the referee said, awarding Hammes the first points.

I didn't panic. I quickly moved to the right, to the left – then forward and backward – moving whatever way I could to break free from his grasp. Several times I felt as if I would get loose, but I couldn't break free. He held me down until the referee's whistle blew again, signaling the end of the first two-minute period.

Hammes led 2-0.

I remained confident. Confident because I could sense that Hammes would not be able to hold me down much longer. He had used up a lot of energy and was panting loudly, trying to get more oxygen into his lungs. He was showing signs of fatigue and I wasn't tired at all. The first period merely got me warmed up.

The referee tossed his red and green coin into the air before we began the second period. It landed with the red side facing up. I wore the red anklet so the referee turned to me and said, "Your choice red, up or down?"

"I'll take down," I said, figuring that Hammes was wearing himself out trying to ride me. If I could escape from him, I would get one point. Then, if I scored the next takedown I would have a 3-2 lead.

When the second round started, I struggled beneath Hammes' long arms and legs once again. I kept my composure and continued to move without stopping. He would have to be in awesome shape to keep me down.

I'm going to get free. I'm going to beat you into the ground, Hammes.

I was determined to get free, but thirty seconds into the second period I still couldn't find an opening. Then, after a quick flurry of movements on the ground, I struggled to my feet once again. I felt Hammes pushing against my back with his chest in a way that I might be able to upset his balance. Even though he was behind me, I could sense his next movement in my own body. I pushed back into him and felt how unsteady he was. If I acted quickly I could toss him to his back, but I had to move NOW, before he could improve his position.

I turned slightly and laced my left arm over his right. I moved in a circle with my feet, arched my hips and threw my whole body into his. The crowd screamed.

The move worked so well that Hammes was fighting to stay in the match. He was on his back. I covered his chest, applying pressure in order to force his shoulder blades to the mat. The referee's hand moved back and forth, counting the seconds I held him down so he could award the right number of near-fall points. If I held him on his back for five seconds, I would earn three points. Those three points combined with the two I had already been awarded for scoring a reversal would give me a comfortable lead, making the score 5-2.

But I didn't want to beat Hammes by outscoring him; I wanted to pin his shoulders to the mat and end the bout. With all my might I pushed his left shoulder blade toward the painted surface. He struggled to survive. The harder he strained, the harder I pushed and the deeper he fell into danger. I could hear the crowd cheering loudly. Some were saying, "GET UP TERRY. FIGHT OFF YOUR BACK, TERRY."

Others were screaming, "STICK HIM FUREY, STICK HIM. PIN HIM."

I looked at the clock as I pushed on him. 25 seconds remained in the period. I imagined my chest pushing right through his body and into the mat, literally crushing him into the ground. This visualization helped me intensify the pressure.

Strength and endurance drained out of Hammes body with each tick of the clock. I was getting closer and closer to hearing the match-ending clap the referee makes to signal a match won by pin.

Come on ref, the sonofabitch is pinned. What the hell are you looking for?

The referee held his head along the side of the mat, making certain no space remained between the mat and Hammes' shoulders. And then Hammes collapsed.

SLAP. The referee whacked the mat with his right palm and blew his whistle to signal the end of the bout. I had defeated my first opponent by pin in 3:43.

I jumped up, raised my hands in the air and shouted "ALLLRIIGHT." The referee quickly brought our hands together. Hammes and I shook hands to display good sportsmanship and the referee rose my hand high in the air, showing the crowd who the winner of the match on Mat 5 was.

A photographer stood in my corner taking shots of me. I looked straight into the camera's lens, put my tongue up to my teeth as if I had finished eating cold nails for breakfast, then ran off the mat in triumph. Coach Greenfield shook my hand and said, "That's one down. You had to win that match in order to place. Good job. Now go have a seat, and get something to eat."

I found a place in the stands a few rows up from Mat 5. My parents came over from their seats to congratulate me on my performance. They sat to my left. My mother handed me a sandwich. To my right sat Dennis O'Grady, a blunt Irishman with light wavy brown hair and circular framed wire-rim glasses. He was the sports editor for my hometown newspaper, **The Times Herald** – and he held a pencil and spiral bound pocket-size notepad in his hands.

"Congratulations, Matt," he said, and before I could say thanks he added, "Tomorrow you face the state champion?" I stared back at him with focused intensity and a fierce look in my eyes, looked down at my shoe laces, began untying them, then said, "He's not this year's state champion yet." O'Grady wrote down my words and said no more. Conversation terminated. He had all he needed for his story.

After he left, I sat and talked with my parents. But as I did I thought about what I said to O'Grady. I had a certain feeling that my words with him, which would appear in the paper the next day, would either make me look extremely confident of my abilities or amazingly stupid about my chances of beating Wayne Love. Maybe both. Most people, if they would have heard me say what I said, would have laughed. My words were a joke. Everyone knew Love was unbeatable.

* * * * *

In the early evening, as I prepared for sleep, my mind drifted back to a conversation I heard four days earlier, when I was riding in a car with Coach Greenfield and another coach, Ray Hawg, the mentor at the public high school in my hometown. Together with Hawg's two state qualifiers, Larry Hurd and

Todd Hammen, we were riding to a small farm town some 26 miles outside of Carroll, called Coon Rapids.

On the morning of that same day, everyone in the car excitedly read the state wrestling pairings in the sports section of **The Des Moines Register**. We knew who I would face if I won my first-round match.

When I woke up that morning I told my mom about a dream I just had. "Mom," I said, "I just dreamt that I pinned Wayne Love at the state tournament. It was incredible."

"Oh my goodness. That's a message from God," she said, hugging me close. "Now keep this dream to yourself. Don't broadcast it to anyone. Lock the emotion inside and let it grow."

I did as my mother suggested. I kept my dream private. My actions would do the talking.

But Coach Hawg had already calculated who the winners in each weight class were going to be. According to him I was predestined to lose.

Loud enough for me and everyone else to hear, he told Coach Greenfield, "At 167, Love's gonna be in the finals. No doubt about it. Love is unstoppable. He's the unbeatable man."

I sat quietly in the back seat, maintaining an external state of calmness while silently exploding expletives off the back of his head. *I'm going to be in the finals,* I said to myself, *not Love. You're an asshole Hawg and I can't wait for you to find out how wrong you are.*

It was hard to sleep when I thought about my forthcoming match with Love. Maybe I had no chance, but the image in my mind told a different story. I saw myself winning. I had no idea how, but that's what I believed.

Tomorrow afternoon, when I dethrone Love the whole state is going to freak, they're going to be in shock.

Now get some sleep.

Furey enroute to pinning Terry Hammes in round one of the State Championships.

Four

When I woke up Friday morning I could feel it in my bones. I was going to make history in a positive way. I was going to dethrone the defending state champion. I was going to beat the unbeatable man, Wayne Love.

My body was relaxed with no trace of soreness. No wounds from yesterday's battle followed me into today's war.

I walked around the floor of my hotel room, stretched my back and loosened my neck.

Today is my day. That's what I kept saying to myself.

Outside the door, **The Des Moines Register** laid waiting on the carpet. I snatched it and quickly flipped to the sport's page. The team standings from day one of the tournament were on page one, and on page three, I found what I was looking for: "Matt Furey of Carroll Kuemper pinned Terry Hammes of Fairfield in 3:43."

As I read the news a rush of energy flooded my body. I held the paper, closed my eyes and gave thanks.

Thank you, God, for making me into a winner. Thanks for helping me prove I'm not a loser. Thanks for the victory yesterday. Please help me again today. I'll be going up against last year's state champion, Wayne Love. Please give me the courage to wrestle him to the best of my ability. Please keep me free from injury. Help me to wrestle him with the same level of confidence I would have against someone I know I can beat.

At 10 o'clock, when I was sitting on my bed, once again, I imagined myself defeating Love. I formed a mental picture of the result I wanted to create, then I increased the intensity of the image by envisioning myself standing head and shoulders taller than Love. I imagined that I was at least 10 feet tall. I imagined Love as if he were half my size. I imagined that my muscles were bigger than his and I mentally choreographed every move I would make against him. The more I pictured beating Love the more psyched up I became.

Love was going to fall.

Right after completing my mental preparations, Coach Greenfield came into the room, started packing his briefcase and said, "You know Matt, we can go watch the semi-finals tonight, if you want."

Go watch the semi-finals. I'm going to be in them.

I held my lips together and pretended I didn't hear him, keeping my mind focused and concentrated on victory. Seeing that my unspoken reaction was different from what was expected, he altered his message and said, "Well, you might be in the semi-finals tonight."

"That's right," I said with conviction. "I'm going to pull off an upset."

Although he tried to hide it, I saw Coach Greenfield roll his eyes up and to the left. As much as he wanted to, he didn't share my belief. What I thought was inevitable he thought impossible - and I couldn't blame him. No one wants to see the people you care about fail; and fail miserably.

I was bold. I was crazy. It was time for me to come down from Cloud 9.

But this match was different from all other matches. I wanted to win and I didn't have room to entertain anyone else's idea about the forthcoming result. I didn't care whether or not my desire was possible. I wanted to be a state champion. I wanted to win. Even if Wayne Love was Superman, I was determined to beat him.

* * * * *

When we arrived at the auditorium about an hour and a half before the quarterfinals began, I ran out on the mat and started to warm up by shadow wrestling, the ultimate way to physically and mentally prepare oneself for battle.

The mats were crowded with the winners from last night's matches. Larry Hurd and Todd Hammen, from Carroll High, the public high school in my hometown, were not there. They lost their first round matches and could only hope that the winner of their bouts advanced to the semi-finals, so they could still come back and place in the top six. I was the only remaining athlete from my hometown that was still competing.

After warming up I went to the training room and sat on the table to get my right ankle taped by one of the trainers. Having my ankle taped was crucial to my performance because of what happened to me nine days earlier.

On a Wednesday afternoon, three days before the district tournament, I was running outside with the team. Toward the end of the run I stepped on a jagged rock and sprained my ankle. Somehow I managed to limp the remaining half-mile back to the wrestling room. In order to convince myself that I wasn't really hurt, I tried to practice some moves with my younger brother, Tim, a freshman. But the ankle was hurt badly, and the pain was unbearable.

When I woke up the next morning my ankle was swollen and the pain was excruciating. I couldn't put weight on my foot without cringing. I couldn't walk.

Duke, a close friend of the family, and a doctor, was at our house eating breakfast with my parents. He ate breakfast at our house almost every morning so that he and my father could discuss politics. And before I left for school each day, Duke, my mother and father and I stood in a circle in the living room and prayed for my wrestling success.

"We're going to get a pipeline of grace streamlined to you from the Almighty," Duke used to say. He was a Protestant. And although we were Catholics, we had no trouble accepting his colloquial manner of talking about God.

Duke always closed his eyes and bowed his head when he prayed, and we did the opposite. Our prayer circle was always permeated by the smell of bacon, eggs and toast – as well as the cigar smoke still lingering on Duke's clothes. He was an affable man whose voice sounded like the quack of a duck. He delivered babies when he wasn't talking politics, but was also known to combine the two on occasion. His hair was thick and grey and his face always had a paradoxical look that made him appear cheerful while he bashed U.S. politicians for being outright communists, or at the least, "wannabe" commies who also happened to be members of the Trilateral Commission and the Council on Foreign Relations (he had the charts and graphs to prove it, too). And although he swore with dynamism and charm, he was always careful not to mix his unholy words with his prayers – at least not around my mom and dad.

But on this particular morning, when Duke saw the swollen flesh surrounding my ankle, he placed praying on the shelf and said, "Goddamnit, we need to take the boy to the hospital. I know the son's a bitches there, especially the physical therapist, Dan Mack. Let's go see what the hell he can do for the boy."

My father, a lawyer, agreed. In his mind there are only three professionals on earth who know anything. Priests ranked number one and after attorneys he put his faith in doctors. So my father and Duke hoisted me into the car, while my mother, a nurse, stayed home and prayed for a miracle.

"We have an all-American boy here that's needs your help," Duke said to the receptionist in the emergency unit of the hospital. "The boy sprained his ankle and he has an important rasslin' tournament on Saturday. We need to put modern medicine to work and get the boy's ankle ready. He can come in all day today and all day tomorrow. Is Dan Mack in?"

"Yes, he is," said the receptionist. "We'll take you into the physical therapy unit. It's still early so he should be available."

The receptionist called another nurse who brought me a wheel chair. Duke took the wheel chair from the nurse and wheeled me down the corridor. All the way to the physical therapy unit, he greeted everyone he saw and said, "This boy's Matt Furey, an all-American rassler. He's hurt but we'll have him ready by Saturday."

My dad, who is typically pensive unless he's talking about God or politics, let Duke do all the talking up to that point, but when Dan Mack came out he managed to say a few words. My father's bald head was an embarrassed shade of pinkish-red and although he wanted to appear as if he was full of hope, when he finally spoke his 5'4" body shrunk to 5'2" and his typically demonstrative authoritarian lawyer voice sounded sad and distraught.

"Matt, he... he's been looking forward to this moment... he's been training for this moment for the past four years. He, he..."

"The boys a damn all-American. He's gonna be famous someday," Duke said, letting my father keep his feelings hidden. "He has two days to go before the district tournament. Hell, you can get him ready by then, can't you?"

Dan Mack took hold of my swollen right ankle and compared it to the left one. "Is it painful?" he asked.

"Damn right it is," said Duke. "The boy can't walk."

"How much does it hurt?" Dan Mack asked again.

"A lot," I said.

"Well, what do you think? Can you get him ready?" Duke questioned.

Dan Mack moved my ankle in every direction, checking me for mobility. Then looked up and said, "I believe we can. Can you leave him here all morning?"

"He's all yours until Saturday morning," Duke said.

For the next two days, Dan Mack and his assistants worked on my ankle. Throughout the morning and afternoon, my ankle took turns getting treated with ice and ultra-sound. Fifteen minutes of ice, fifteen minutes of ultra-sound, and a half-hour of rest with my leg elevated and tightly wrapped in an ace bandage.

While I rested on a padded table Dan Mack and I talked about wrestling.

"Do you have any weight you need to drop for the tournament?" he asked.

"No, my weight is fine," I said.

"That's good. It would be difficult for you to cut weight if you can't run it off like most wrestlers have to do," he said.

"That's true," I said.

"What do you do to keep your weight down?" he questioned.

"I didn't go out for football. I spent the entire fall getting my weight down so that I wouldn't bounce up and down during the season. I was 187 pounds when I started reducing. Now I weigh in most days at 167, so I don't need to cut an ounce – and that's a big change from previous years when I had to drop several pounds within the last 24 hours to make weight."

"Really? That's great. Did you follow a special diet?"

"I eat meat and eggs and stay away from all the refined foods, especially bread and pasta. My mom told me they make you fat. No one else on the team believed me and they can't control their weight. I've found it's a lot easier to control my weight without all that starch."

"Sounds like you've got a lot of self-discipline," Mack said.

"I do my best," I said.

"Well, I'm from Waterloo, you know. And Waterloo always turns out the best wrestlers in the state and oftentimes the best in the nation," Mack said.

"Yeah, I know," I said.

"You know Dan Gable?" he questioned.

"Of course, he's my idol," I said.

"Well, I watched Gable compete when he was in high school. Then I followed him at Iowa State and in the Olympics. You'll never find a better wrestler than Gable to come out of Waterloo," he said.

"I know. Every year I read a biography written about him for extra-inspiration."

"Which one do you read?"

"It's called **The Legend of Dan Gable, The Wrestler** – by Russ L. Smith," I said.

"Really, I'll have to get that one and read it. Russ L. Smith writes for **The Waterloo Courier**, so that must be a good one. I'll bet the book is motivating."

"It sure is," I said.

"Do you know some of the other wrestlers from Waterloo?" Mack asked.

"Not too many," I said.

"Well, one of Gable's assistants at Iowa is from Waterloo. His name is Chuck Yagla. He won two national titles for Iowa and even made it on the Olympic team in 1980, but of course we didn't go because of President Carter's boycott. And then there are a couple brothers from Waterloo: Bob and Don Buzzard. I'll tell you, they're the meanest wrestlers I ever saw."

"I heard about them," I said.

"And then there is Dale Anderson. He's another two-time national champion from Waterloo. I think he is a law professor now."

"My dad will like hearing that. He always wants to know who the smartest champion wrestlers are. He's working on a theory that a large percentage of champion wrestlers have higher I.Q.'s than most people."

"In that case he should know how smart Chuck Yagla is. How many people do you know who had a perfect score on their SAT?"

"I don't know anyone who did. That's amazing. A perfect score on his SAT."

"Matt, have you heard about the new star wrestler from Waterloo? His name is Wayne Love. Do you know him?"

"Uh, yeah. We're in the same weight class this year," I said.

"Really? Well, all I can say is GOOD LUCK. Man, he's tough. He's the defending state champion. He beat his opponent in the finals last year by so many points you'd think it was a match against a five-year old. But not only that, he was all-state as a running back in football and I think he's also a state champion in the 100-meter dash."

"He's an animal," I said. "But I'm not in this to lose – so stupid as it sounds to some, if he gets between me and a state title – I'm not going to lie down and let him win. He's going to be in for the fight of his life."

"I better really work to get you healthy by Saturday," said Dan Mack. "You're going to need to be 100% when you wrestle him at the state meet."

Other than during my stay in the physical therapy unit, I never spoke about my desire to dethrone Love as state champion to anyone. I figured Duke had done enough talking for me – and besides, too much talk before the fact sort of takes the place of *doing* something, especially if a lot of people give you praise for your desire. If you tell someone your goals and they say, "Wow, that's great!" you've got to be careful. Pats on the back before accomplishment tend to clog your desire to actually make the goal happen. At least that's my theory.

And if my ankle didn't heal, there would be no state championship tournament for me. So the best thing I could do was keep quiet and focus all my energy on healing my ankle. My only chances rested in the hands of Dan Mack and in how I used my mind to heal the injury. I would have to use every cell of mental power to get my ankle ready in two days. It was better for me to keep quiet and picture my goals as an accomplished fact. And so, as I rested in the physical therapy unit those two days, I never allowed the thought of not being able to compete in the state meet enter my mind. There was no second chance. I was 100 percent committed. That's why I felt absolutely certain I would be ready to wrestle in the district meet on Saturday. My ankle would be healthy. I was determined to make it so.

Two days later, I got on the team bus with crutches beneath my arms. My teammates looked at me wondering what I was going to do. One of them, Pat, a 145-pounder, asked what all of them wanted to know: "Are you going to wrestle today?"

"Yes," I said.

"But how?" he replied.

"Watch me and you'll find out," I said.

When the district tournament began, my ankle was ready. I won my first two matches; the first by pin and the second 8-4. Once I reached the finals I knew I had already qualified for the state meet. And because I didn't want to re-injure my ankle before the state tournament, I played it safe in the finals and let my opponent, Jim Sturdevant, of Fort Dodge, take the match by a 7-2 margin. The health of my ankle was more important to me in that match than whether I won or lost. My first goal had already been fulfilled. A more important goal, winning the state title, was a week away, and it was important to take no unnecessary risks.

And so, before my quarterfinal match in the state tournament with Wayne Love, as I sat and watched the female trainer taping a tight figure-8 around my ankle as if it were no more complicated than combing her own hair, I thought about my injury, my one area of vulnerability, my Achilles' heel. I wondered if it were possible for Wayne Love, with all his power, strength, speed and grace to have an area of weakness. Was it possible for him to get hurt? To sprain an ankle? To tear cartilage in his knee?

I couldn't see it. He was too awesome. Yet somehow, I believed that I, an unknown, an underdog, could defeat this powerful, formidable, seemingly unbeatable foe.

I took these thoughts into the stands where I began to concentrate on what I wanted to make happen in my upcoming bout.

It was a long wait before my weight class was up, so I sat and concentrated deeply as each match from 98 to 138 pounds was called. Hearing the 145-pound class would serve as my signal to get up, get moving and get ready for battle.

Five

I left the stands and started warming up in a place I began to think of as "my corner."

I was not alone in this corner. How could I be? There were hundreds of wrestlers in the auditorium, who like me, needed to warm up. From almost every city someone was representing their hometown and their high school. Each of these wrestlers looked like a total stud. And he was, to some degree, otherwise he wouldn't have been at the state meet. Each wrestler had a fire, a spirit in him that did not want to be extinguished.

I jumped around and shook every muscle in my body to get ready. Then I stretched and mentally rehearsed every move I needed to use in the most important match of my career.

I shadow wrestled, moving forward, circling, gesticulating with my arms, fainting with my head and upper body, stalking an invisible opponent who would become visible to me in a few minutes. I pictured Wayne Love in front of me and envisioned the moves I wanted to see materialize. I felt each move inside my body as if I were in a dream I couldn't awaken from; a dream I didn't want to wake up from. The sensations I was feeling were a mental high I didn't want to come down from.

My imaginings were interrupted every few minutes by the tournament announcer who told the crowd the results of matches that had finished. I pondered what the announcer would be saying about me after my match with Love. Would I be the victor? Or would I get pummeled, thrashed and beaten?

Time for dwelling on this thought ended when the call for my match rang over the loud speakers: "WAYNE LOVE OF WATERLOO CENTRAL VERSUS

MATT FUREY OF CARROLL KUEMPER, ON DECK MAT TWO. LOVE AND FUREY, REPORT TO MAT TWO."

Zero Time. Time when preparation meets opportunity. Time for two athletes, Wayne and me.

I ran to the corner of Mat 2 with Coach Greenfield, who matched me stride-for-stride. This was the first time I saw him run so hard and even though he basically told me he expected me to lose, he went to my corner and cheered me on like I was going to win. Perhaps he picked up on my intention and came to believe what I told him at the hotel.

One thing is certain, I was Greenfield's chance to say, "I coached a state champion." He had previously coached a 185-pounder to the state finals when he was at another school, but the athlete ended up taking second place. Coach Greenfield could avenge that loss through me.

Throughout the tournament he kept telling me how I needed to win my first match in order to place, but he knew that placing wasn't good enough for me. Deep inside every coach and inside every wrestler is the desire to win it all, to say you are the best. I was going up against someone who could claim to be the best and I could never make a claim like this myself unless I defeated Love, which would put me one step closer to the finals.

It may have been impossible for Coach Greenfield to approach this match with the same enthusiasm and faith I had. But no matter what he thought, he could still fake it. To do otherwise would be a sign of weakness, a signal that he wasn't a good coach. I had faith in Coach Greenfield and nothing was more important to me than the respect he gave me at that moment. If he could maintain this enthusiasm for me as the match progressed, regardless of what the score reflected, it would be easier to accept a loss. Nothing is worse, nothing so disturbing as being the wrestler who endures the silence of his coaches and fans as they mentally throw in the towel for you, giving up all hope.

Coach Greenfield, in this match, would be the coach I wanted and needed. He would cheer and scream. He would give unconditional support to the wrestler who, until now, had won 22 matches for him while losing only five. A record that was good by most people's standards, but to someone like Love, who was unbeaten, not only this year, but the year before as well, and almost the year before that, too – my record was a joke. I doubt that Love took me seriously. And if he'd have known my overall record in high school, he might have laughed at me when we shook hands.

As a freshman 138-pounder, I was 10-0 against those in the same grade. But after the varsity man quit I was asked to fill in, otherwise there would be a hole in the roster. I did so and got pummeled match after match. I won once and lost eleven times – ending the season with a combined record of 11 wins and 11 losses.

My sophomore year I moved up to 155 pounds. I went 5-7 for the season, wrestling mostly against juniors and seniors.

My junior year started out great but ended up poorly. Overall, I was 16-8 – and a first-round loser in the district tournament.

Now, as a senior, after starting out the season 7-4, I got on a roll and won 14 straight matches. My only loss in a couple months was the finals of the district tournament. And here I was, with an overall dismal high school record, bold enough and gutsy enough to think I had a chance to beat someone whom others believed could rip my head from my body.

* * * * *

The referee called us forward to begin the match.

He handed me the red ankle band, (the same color I wore in the first bout) and gave Love the green one.

I got the lucky color, I thought as I wrapped the velcro band around my ankle to signal that the time for talking was over. Love and I would be on fighting terms for the next six minutes.

Love walked to the center of the mat and took his stance. He looked a foot taller than me. His right biceps jumped as we shook hands. *Damn, this guy's freakin huge.*

When the referee blew his whistle to start the match, I must have looked like a tortoise who wanted to pop back into his shell. Before I could blink, Love hit me with a lightning-fast double-leg takedown that shook my spine like an earthquake. Now I knew why he won the 100 meters and was a first-team all-state running back. Within two seconds of the first period, I was behind, 2-0, and I couldn't help but think I was in for a thrashing.

My God, this guy is quicker and stronger than anyone I have ever seen. If he can score on me this fast, I'll be lucky to survive.

After the first two minutes Love still led 2-0, and I didn't give him any indication that I was going to be tough. He was never off balance and I was definitely not a threat. He was in complete control.

In my opening match against Hammes I was trailing 2-0, too, but at least I felt like I could move, that I had opportunities to score. Against Love… NOTHING. I felt like an invalid… unable to move a muscle without his consent.

During the second two-minute period I started in the top position. The referee blew his whistle, and, KABOOM – Love exploded out of my grasp like a rocket being launched to the moon. He spun around so fast everything went blurry and fuzzy on me – then he immediately smashed through me with another double-leg takedown. I was now losing 5-0.

God, help me. I'm getting mauled.

For some strange reason, as I crawled to my base, sweat dripping under the pounding I was enduring, I recalled my only other competition against a state champion.

A year earlier I wrestled Steve Ross, of Ames. In that match, after he effortlessly racked up a 13-point lead, he pinned me in front of my hometown fans. It was the most humiliating defeat of my life – and Ross went on to win the state title a few months later.

Now I was losing 5-0 and reliving the same thoughts of getting humiliated – and I didn't like it one bit. The current score reminded me of the former loss and the comparison made me think about how wimpy I was. And this thought triggered something inside me that made me get royally pissed off. A fury built up within and it was time to let it out.

Is this how you want to spend the rest of your career? Do you want to spend the rest of your life afraid to give your best against someone because he's better than you – or because he's a state champion?

When I asked myself these questions I got even angrier. Angry enough to burst.

A surge of power came over me. Inside I felt as powerful as a grizzly – and I began to work to free myself from Love's mighty grasp. But grizzly strength or not, for a spell, I was still trapped and going nowhere; trapped until the referee noticed something I couldn't see.

The referee could see me making a massive effort to get free. At the same time he saw Love dogging it, taking his time, coasting, no longer trying to score points. He was content to loaf through the match. I was the tortoise, he was the hare, and until now, I was no threat to his 5-point lead.

You can't coast in a wrestling match, though. It's a penalty we classify as stalling. The first time a referee notices your stalling tactics, you receive a warning. If the stalling continues he starts awarding penalty points to the person who is enduring the stalling. In this case, that was ME.

When a match is refereed correctly, no wrestler, including those who are state champions, is allowed to stall. You are expected to try and dominate your opponent from start to finish. Wayne Love started out in dominating fashion, but when 45 seconds remained in the second period, my relentless attempt to get free was draining him of energy. He wanted the victory to be easy. But something snapped within and I wasn't the same guy who took the mat a couple minutes earlier.

The referee took note.

"Warning green (Love). I have a warning for stalling on green. Work up on him green. Work for the pin green, you can't just hold onto him," the referee said.

Love picked up his pace for a few moments, showing the ref how hard he was working. But after twenty more seconds he returned to his tortoise-and-hare game. Maybe he figured the ref wasn't serious. He wouldn't penalize a defending state champ, would he? And with a 5-0 lead, it didn't matter if he lost a point, did it?

The second period ended with no change in the score. I only had two more minutes to fix that.

I started the third period in the down position, a familiar spot for me. I had been in that position for all but a few seconds of the entire match. Love took the top position and within seconds of hearing the referee's whistle, he laced his left leg inside of mine and grabbed onto my right arm, trying to break me down so he could turn me to my back in a move called the guillotine. I countered his move by locking my hands.

For twenty seconds we struggled for better position, and then I was the only one struggling and Love was loafing again. He knew I couldn't get out of his hold, even if I wasn't on my back. Why shouldn't he continue to coast?

But as soon as he began to loaf the referee nailed him for stalling. He would show no favoritism.

"I have stalling on green," the ref said. "One point for red."

My first point against the state champion. I finally scored. YES!

When I received my first point Coach Greenfield started yelling at me through his habitually cupped hands. "HE'S TIRED MATT. HE'S TIRED. KEEP GOING. HE CAN'T KEEP UP WITH YOUR PACE ANYMORE."

Compared to some of my other matches, I didn't look like I was wrestling a hard pace because so much of the effort could not be seen with quick, flashy movements.

But my coach was right. Love was really getting tired. I remembered the thoughts I had about Achilles' heels when my ankle was getting taped. Had we found the Achilles' heel of the man who was unbeatable? My God, he DID have a weakness after all. He wasn't in as good of shape as I was.

My conditioning was excellent, and many of my matches were won through superior stamina alone. I wore my opponents down, but I never thought I could wear the state champion down. Champions didn't get tired, right? Especially when they appeared to be winning so easily.

The reality was that Love was tired and his bout with me was tougher than most. The old saying, "conditioning is your best hold" was ringing truer with every second. With each tick of the clock Love was getting more exhausted and his technique sloppier than before. On the other hand, my technique was beginning to look sharper than it had ever been. What a change!

Making things even worse for Love, the referee was finding it easier to penalize him.

When the score changed to 5-1, Love still didn't seem worried. He kept right on doing what he was doing: giving occasional bursts of effort to make it look like he was trying, then resting to recover his wind. He must have figured I didn't have the time to score enough points to win.

Only 60 seconds remained in the match and I was still underneath Love – unable to break away from him. Love must have thought, "How can I possibly lose? I'm up by four and this guy can't score."

Maybe he didn't sense that I was getting stronger and more determined. He probably didn't know that my skills improved in direct proportion to the length of the bout. He didn't know that I always won the close bouts when conditioning was the only critical factor separating the spread of points. All Love knew was that he wanted the match over with.

I didn't have the same idea in mind. Love would really have to work his ass off for the last 60 seconds of the match. If he didn't he was going to regret it.

Keeping his leg laced inside mine and hovering over me like a flea that couldn't be shaken off, Love continued to make no attempts to advance his position. The referee wouldn't tolerate this tactic and with 45 seconds remaining in the match, he blew his whistle to stop the action.

"I have another warning for stalling on green. One point red."

The score was now 5-2.

I felt that killer instinct, that fury on the mat take hold of me and when the referee started the match again, I exploded to my feet just like Love had done earlier in the match. To my utter amazement, this time Love's mighty grip released and I was free.

"One point escape, red. One point red," the referee yelled, pointing one finger in the air.

5-3.

0:30.

Love charged after me. He grabbed onto my head and neck and pushed against my collarbone with every bit of strength remaining in his body. My 5'8" frame pushed back against all six-feet of his. As we locked horns and pushed, he backed up a few steps and I launched into one of my favorite moves, the fireman's carry. I scooped Love off the mat and landed on him.

Takedown Furey, two points. Right?

Wrong???

The referee didn't give me two points for the takedown. He blew his whistle instead. The action stopped and the crowd sat in silent wonder. Love and I were called to our feet. Then the referee said, "I have stalling again on green. Two points red."

"What?" Love said, questioning the ref's call.

"You backed up a step before he shot in on you," said the referee. "Now you better start wrestling and keep moving forward or else you're going to be disqualified."

Locking horns with Wayne Love in the quarter finals.

I couldn't believe what was happening. The two points made the score 5-5.

"OH MY GOD. THIS IS UNBELIEVABLE," screamed a cheerleader sitting by the mat next to Coach Greenfield.

"MATT. YOU CAN DO IT. YOU CAN WIN," Greenfield yelled, no longer seeing my prediction as wishful thinking.

0:17 remained.

The entire crowd of 15,000 stood in awe. With eyes glued on Love and me, they were seeing history in the making. No one had given Love a close match in two years. Everyone he wrestled had been beaten like a drum. Everyone but me.

My body shook with anticipation of the referee's signal. I now had more energy than when the bout began. I envisioned the move I wanted to use to win the match and when the referee's silver sound piece blew I stalked Love like a wolverine. I was on a one-man stampede. I lunged forward, attacking both of Love's legs at the knees. I hit my double-leg takedown with every ounce of strength and speed I could summon. It was the most incredible double-leg I'd ever shot in my life. It was the same move Love had used on me to begin the match.

BAAAAAM!

Love went down. Down to his back. I counted the points to myself as I went for the pin.

Two-point takedown, Furey. Three-point nearfall, Furey. Victory is mine. I'm winning 10-5.

Yes, I was. I had to be. But then…. the referee's whistle blew again, stopping the action.

What the hell is going on?

The man in the zebra shirt then uttered the following unforgettable phrases:

"No takedown. No back points. I have a final warning for stalling on green. You're disqualified."

"I'm what?" said Love in disbelief.

"You backed up again before he attempted his last move," the referee replied.

WOOOOOOOW! I WON. I WON. I JUST BEAT THE STATE CHAMP!!!.

The referee pulled our hands together, held onto both of our wrists and raised my right hand toward the heavens. Love looked down, dejectedly. I looked up, full of elation and started running around the mat, overcome with emotion. I saw three of my teammates sitting in the front row. I didn't know they were there to watch. They were jumping up and down, yelling my name, "FUREY, FUREY, FUREY," over and over.

"He's last year's state champ now," I said. "I told everyone what he was and they laughed. I beat the champ. I beat the champ. I just beat the unbeatable man."

"We always knew you could do it," said a cheerleader who came over to hug me.

I ran over to Coach Greenfield who was standing in our corner, excitedly rubbing his hands on his face. He stretched out his arms, grabbed me in a bear hug and picked me up off the ground. Although he only weighed about 130 pounds, he squeezed me with the power of an 800-pound gorilla.

I had done the unthinkable, the unfathomable, the unimaginable. I had beaten Wayne Love. "Last year's state champ."

Love was disqualified with only thirteen seconds remaining. Never before, in the history of the Iowa State High School Wrestling Championships had a defending champion lost by disqualification. I would be in the semi-finals that evening. Love, not me, would be watching from the stands. My afternoon fortune telling was on target and my dismal overall high school record was now a thing of the past. I just went from nobody to somebody.

Trying to control Wayne Love is no easy task.

Six

After my victory over Love, people I didn't know and had never met before came out of the stands to congratulate me. And people who did know me ran up to hug me or shake my hand. My parents were there, too. As soon as the match ended my 5'1" and 105-pound mother ran down the stairs from the upper level like an Olympic sprinter doing the high-hurdles.

"Oh Matt. You were so terrific. I'm so proud of you. I prayed so hard for you. God is so good to you. This is so wonderful. I've got to go call your brothers and Uncle Jack. They'll be so happy."

My mom's wavy black hair was still in place despite her sprint to the floor and she was still holding her rosary when she hugged me. Saying the rosary was the habit that helped her maintain her composure in the insane atmosphere of a wrestling match. And no matter where I wrestled, my mother was always sitting directly above me, in the middle of the stands. From this vantage point she continually moved her lips while kneading her beads. As she held the beads between her thumb and index finger, she somehow managed to simultaneously scream and pray for me.

My dad was much more reserved. I suppose attorneys are cautious in everything they do, even when showing affection to their children. It was always easier for dad to ask questions than it was for him to make statements, unless, of course, his statements were as significant as the closing argument presented to a jury.

My dad was the one who helped ignite the spark of desire in me to become a champion. Most of his life was spent in the living room of our house, where he sat in his favorite green chair... reading. My dad never spent much time talking to me but occasionally, when he had a few questions to ask, he knew the exact buttons to push to motivate me.

"You gonna let those big city school kids whoop you next year?" he'd ask when he saw me getting ready to work out.

"No, I'm not," I'd respond.

"You sure?"

"I'm sure."

"Good. That's what I like to hear."

In my first three years of high school I frequently lost to guys from the big city schools my dad referred to, but this year was different. I was beating the guys from big city schools, and I just beat a guy from Waterloo, the most prestigious wrestling city in the nation.

When my mom left to make phone calls to relatives about my victory, my dad stepped in and hugged me tight, something he rarely did. Then in a commanding voice, he said, "Matt – you're doing great. We're so proud of you. Keep it up. Only two more matches to go for you to win the title."

"You got it," I said.

"Just one question for you though, Matt. I noticed when the match started that Love took you down before you knew what happened."

"Yeah, yeah, yeah."

"Well, I was wondering, is there something you can do to keep that from happening again? You looked like you weren't concentrating. But only for a second. Isn't there something you can do to guard against that in the future?"

My younger brother Tim interrupted my dad to congratulate me. I asked him what he thought of the match and he told me he didn't see it. He wouldn't explain why. Later on I found out from my mother that he was afraid to watch my matches because he believed that when he did, he somehow jinxed me. He thought his presence brought bad luck my way.

When I looked at my brother I couldn't find anything about him that could bring misfortune upon me. His belief was only a superstition, but who was I to knock superstition, when I had a ton of quirks myself?

I guess this one took me by surprise because Tim had watched me win many matches before. But now, for some peculiar reason, he carried a notion that didn't make sense. At the same time, though, I could see why he did it. It was his odd way of saying that he was rooting for me and that he was afraid to see me lose.

In my match with Love, it didn't take long for Tim to hear the results of the match. He didn't have to wait to hear about them from the announcer. He could hear them in the hallways, where he nervously sat eating popcorn. The crowd was so loud during my match that Tim could barely maintain his composure as he sat on the floor intently listening for the results of each match. But as soon as the match ended, he heard people running through the doors, grabbing their friends and excitedly telling them, "Did you see what just happened? Wayne Love got beat. The referee disqualified him for stalling with thirteen seconds left."

Tim immediately burst into tears. He wanted me to succeed so badly. But even though he saw his viewing of my matches as a detriment to my performance, his spirit was with me in the bustling hallways. He deserved as much credit for my victory as I did. He was the one who drilled with me at 5:30 each morning. He was the one who practiced with me every afternoon, after the other wrestlers went home. He was the one who accompanied me to my third and final workout each day, when I did calisthenics and drilled my moves again.

He helped me develop the double-leg takedown that I used in the closing seconds of my match with Love. He was the one who fired me up when I drilled, saying to me, "I bet you can't beat Love. I bet that move won't work against him. I bet he wins it all again."

When he said these words to me I trained harder, more ferociously, determined to prove him wrong.

With such a positive impact on me, how could he possibly think watching my matches would detract from my final outcome? Maybe he felt guilty for always saying I would get beat. Maybe he couldn't bear to face what everyone believed would happen to me. I can only speculate about his reasons. It's a mystery to me and it will always be his secret.

*   *   *   *   *

After visiting with family and friends I told Coach Greenfield I wanted to go back to the hotel, to get away from the crowd. Some wrestlers loved watching everyone else perform, but because I didn't have anyone else still competing from my team or hometown, I preferred solitude. A lot of solitude. Hanging around in the midst of the multitude was emotionally draining. The thought of lying on my back in a private place, staring at the ceiling and contemplating my next victory was what I needed most.

My next opponent would be tough: third-ranked Joe Nekvinda of Cedar Rapids Prairie. Following my victory over Love, the last thing I needed was a letdown against Nekvinda. Beating him would place me in the finals the following evening. I needed to stay focused. Fewer distractions would help me concentrate on the semi-finals. There would be no looking ahead to the finals until after I won. Nekvinda was enough to think about for now.

Take one match at a time. Take one match at a time. That's the key. I kept repeating Coach Greenfield's mantra to myself as we left the auditorium. It was working.

In my hotel room, I stripped off my uniform, jumped in the shower and screamed with excitement as the warm water washed the sweat from my skin. I pounded my fist against the palm of my left hand and yelled, "YES. YES. YES."

What a moment. This is what athletes call "the thrill of victory." For me, it was ecstasy.

For Wayne Love, losing was the agony of defeat. Later that day I heard that he ran into the locker room, screaming, crying – unable to console himself after the loss. I felt a secret sorrow for him, even though, in wrestling, the victor could show no compassion for the vanquished. But even though I felt sorry for Wayne, the pride I felt in my victory was much stronger. His loss to me may have been the most disappointing moment of his life. No one cherishes disappointing moments. I'd had my share of them and I didn't want anymore. Beating Love helped prevent MY own.

Keep striving for the top.. The tournament is far from over. This is what you've worked for and trained for. And how bad Wayne Love feels right now is none of your business. He had just as much chance to beat you, if not more, than you had.

Ruthlessness and a killer instinct were the qualities I would need more of to win the title. There could be no room for compassion when I stepped out on the mat. There's no such thing as "friendship" when you compete against one another in the sport of wrestling. After the match, yes – but not during.

Seven

Following my shower and an hour-long spontaneous wall-staring meditation, Coach Greenfield and I went out to eat. I had my usual pre-match high protein meal: eggs.

Eggs were the food that gave me strength and stamina. I ate so many of them, from the time I was a small boy, that my mother's friends used to say to me, "One of these days you're going to start cackling and turn into a chicken."

Eggs were not the typical food wrestlers were told to eat for energy. Pancakes, toast, potatoes, pasta – yes, these were the high carbohydrates we were told to devour. But eggs were my choice because they were what I had eaten before every victory during the year. I never lost when I had eggs. I ate them before my first two matches in this tournament, and I'd won both of them. So in my superstitious mind, eggs were one of the keys to my success. Don't change a winning game, that was what I was told, and I believed it.

Ritual permeated almost every action on the days I wrestled. Even the days before I wrestled.

I trained the same way the day before each match. I tried my best to think the same thoughts, too. On the day of each match I wore the same blue dress pants and the same blue button down shirt. On the collar of this shirt I wore a gold pin depicting a man headlocking his opponent. I wore the same shoes, the same socks and the same belt. I thought that everything I did had some magical way of structuring and ordering my life – ensuring more victories in the future.

My wrestling gear was no exception. I wore the same gold Kuemper wrestling t-shirt when I warmed up for a match, as well as the same socks and wrestling shoes.

I was emotionally attached to my wrestling shoes. They were white with blue stripes – and were the ONLY change in my wrestling gear all season; a change that was not easy for me to make. My parents, filled with embarrassment, could no longer bare to watch me compete with shoes that were four years old and had tape wrapped around them in order to hold the fabric together. I just could not and would not give them up until the day my entire foot burst through the leather during a match.

After my mother pleaded with me to buy a new pair, I agreed, but only because I believed the new shoes would contribute to my performance; they would bring me new luck. My new shoes were a brand called Asics Tiger. My idol, Dan Gable, had his signature on the side of each manufactured pair, and I couldn't think of anything more auspicious than having his name on the side of my shoes.

As I continued to eat my eggs I silently contemplated my upcoming semi-final bout. This time Coach Greenfield and I kept our thoughts about the match to ourselves. Although I was generally a talkative person, I wasn't when I had wrestling on my mind. Thinking about wrestling was meditation, a time when I was totally transfixed. It gave me inner peace.

Meditation was part of my upbringing. My mother and father spent time each day meditating on the mysteries of the rosary. I did so, too, in order to eradicate my ornery personality. Before going to bed each night I would say a decade of Hail Mary's while fingering the beads draped over the frame of my bed. I always asked for two things: to become a champion wrestler and to become a good person. The more I prayed for the grace to be a good person, the more faults I became aware of, and wrestling gave me a way to fix them.

Wrestling season always helped me become more positive; it gave me a channel to focus my energy. The change to a healthier diet, the periods of time I fasted to control my weight, the hours of practice, and the concentration on a worthwhile goal helped me stay calm and remain optimistic about my future. It sure beat sitting around at home, passively watching television, feeling powerless and out of control.

Everyone who knew me told me they liked me most during wrestling season. One of my high school teachers, Mr. Barton, a pot-bellied man who taught biology and walked on his tip toes, said it in other words. One day during my junior year, when wrestling season had been over for a month, and I no longer had a significant outlet for my high level of energy, he asked me to come out in the hall for a "little chat."

He didn't approve of the way I was talking to a fellow student, a dope smoking farm boy named Peter, whom I hated because he was always telling me how great it was to spend the whole day in school being stoned.

My teacher never heard this student telling me how stupid it was for me to train so hard or how the only people who wrestled were idiots. He never heard him call me a jock who was "all brawn with no brains." He only heard me say, "Listen you ignorant smelly shit-kicking bastard, you're the sorriest excuse for a man that has ever set foot in this high school."

That was why I was called out for a little chat. I knew I was going to hate what Mr. Barton had to say when he called it a chat. The word "chat" always annoyed me. And so did everything else Mr. Barton said to me that day.

"Furey, I'm a man of few words," he began. "Let me put it to you bluntly. Before wrestling season began I thought you were an asshole. During wrestling season I noticed a big change in your personality. I thought you were a really nice guy. But now that wrestling season is over, I think you're an asshole again. That's all I have to say. I'm a man of few words."

Rightly so, I thought.

Eight

Coach Greenfield's wife, Marilyn, and a high school senior named Kristy shared a hotel room next door to ours. Marilyn was even shorter than my mom, with light brownish blond hair that looked like it was about to turn red. She always wore a pair of bluish glasses that fit her easy-going personality perfectly. When you looked at her face you instantly felt you could openly share your darkest secrets or most troubling problems with her and she would hold all of them in confidence.

I loved going to the library in our high school where she worked, and while there I talked to her about wrestling. It wasn't easy finding a woman who liked to talk about wrestling the way a wrestler likes to talk about wrestling, but she was from Waterloo, so she was surrounded by the sport her entire life, even before conception.

Oftentimes, she told me stories about Dan Gable and each one held me spellbound.

"I remember going out on the high school track at Waterloo West to run a couple miles," she told me. "And when I got out there Gable was already running laps around the track. He always wore a lot of sweat clothes and pulled his hood up over his head. I'd stay about twenty or twenty-five minutes and Gable would pass me by several times, running at high speed. I tried to stay out there as long as I could, to get in the shape he was in, but I couldn't. And when I left to go home he was still out there running."

I was so inspired when Marilyn told me a story like this that I would go out to the track at night and run harder than I had ever run before. The next day I would return to the library to hear more.

"What else do you know about Gable?" I asked.

"Well, when he was in high school he used to go around and give clinics with his coach, Bob Siddens," she said.

"Did you ever see any of these clinics?" I asked.

"Oh yeah. Quite a few times."

"And what was Gable like when he was in high school? Was his technique pretty good?"

"He was phenomenal. He was much lighter than he is now. He always wore a crew cut, which made him look mean. And when he demonstrated a move he looked like he could do it on anyone, no matter how big he was."

Whenever we talked in the library, Marilyn knew how to keep me, as well as herself out of trouble. Her boss, a tall blackish-haired lady named Louise, was considered by many to be the terror of the school. If she caught you talking, even whispering in her library she would explode. The kids at school named her Sasquatch, not only because of her height, but because of the way she walked. She usually limped on her right leg and wore a frown that made her look like she just finished a battle in the South Pacific.

Sasquatch hated me when I was a freshman and sophomore, and didn't care for me much as a junior, either. But when I became a senior, Marilyn somehow convinced her that I was an okay guy.

The morning before I left for Des Moines I stopped in the library to talk with Marilyn, and Sasquatch treated me like I was a king. She smiled for the first time in four years, but I suspected it might have been longer because I had only known her for four years.

Prior to this day, and prior to my senior year, Sasquatch threw me out of the library at least once a week for talking, but oftentimes because she *thought* I looked like I might say something. But now things were different. I was her boy, and this was somewhat gratifying because, as far as I could tell, there were no other people in the entire school that she liked.

"Matt, how do you think you'll do in Des Moines?" she asked.

"Oh, I think I'll do quite well," I said with a smile.

"Do you think you'll win?"

"You bet," I replied.

"Aaah, you have such confidence. We'll be praying for you, you know, and we're sure you'll do well, too. After all, you've read every wrestling book in this library at least 10 times."

This was true. In fact, when you looked at the card inserted in each book, my name was the only one listed. Each book bore my signature, marked by the letter "X."

Why the 'X'?

Well, in a business law class, the teacher, Mr. Templemeyer, taught us that if you were illiterate it was perfectly legal to sign your name any way you wanted. "You can even sign your name with the letter "X," Templemeyer said, and I could think of no shorter method of signing my name than that, so I adopted the letter as my trademark signature. Soon afterward other students started imitating the signature, so eventually I modified it in triplicate, signing my name, "XXX."

When I returned to the auditorium in the evening to prepare for my semi-final bout, I felt like Mr. XXX. Everywhere I went people pointed at me and began talking. But they weren't using my name. They weren't saying, "There's Matt Furey. He's a great wrestler from Carroll Kuemper." No. Instead of hearing my name I heard, "There's the guy who beat Wayne Love."

And that's the reality of sport I never figured into my quest. Think of it, I worked my ass off to become known as a great wrestler. I moved in that direction by beating Love, but I wasn't recognized for who I was, and how good I was, but rather for whom I had beaten. This made me know how Larry Owings must have felt.

Larry Owings will always be known as the one guy who beat Dan Gable during Gable's high school and collegiate career. When Gable was a senior in college at Iowa State University, he was already considered a legend. His high school record at Waterloo West was 64-0, with three state titles to his credit. Entering the finals of the national championships during his senior year at Iowa State, his record was an incredible 181-0. His final collegiate match would be a victory, everyone assumed.

He was facing unheralded Larry Owings, a sophomore from Washington State. Only one person believed he was good enough to beat Dan Gable and that person was Owings. He was so confident of his ability to beat Gable, that before the tournament started he told the press he would be the first to conquer the legend. And he did, too, winning the match, 13-11.

I read about the match several times in books about Gable's career, and every time I looked at the picture of Gable standing on step number two of the victory stand, covering his eyes with his right hand, sobbing uncontrollably, chills covered the skin of my body and I felt like crying myself. That's the powerful effect one photo depicting the agony of defeat can have on someone, even decades after the fact.

I didn't like the feeling of only being known as the person who beat Wayne Love, but the reality was I had to live with it, and with two matches remaining for me to claim a state title, I still had a chance to rid myself of the label.

My body continued to flow with energy and enthusiasm from the pride I felt from beating Love in the quarterfinals. The crowd's energy was more intense than the first two rounds, and as I warmed up for my match, I felt like I was absorbing their energy. I didn't feel normal anymore. My body felt as tall as a pine tree and my experience of each moment was amplified to the point that the auditorium itself seemed to have a measurable pulse. I lost sense of time. I was in some sort of mystical trance. Never before, never in my life could I remember feeling so good. I was in the zone and I hoped I could maintain this mental state forever.

Time moved as fast as it always does, but it was slow motion to me. And before it seemed possible, there I was, strapping on my headgear and putting the velcro band around my ankle.

I walked to the inner most center of the mat and shook hands with my opponent, Joe Nekvinda, who had won 25-straight matches; 23 in a row by pin.

No big deal, right?

Hell, after beating Love I expected to trounce Nekvinda, as if he had no talent at all, as if being ranked third in the state didn't mean a damn thing.

Nine

When I shook hands with Nekvinda, for the first time in my career, I felt like a great wrestler. It was a feeling that made my feet dance and my arms dangle with a sensation they never had before. It was a feeling I believed could only be maintained with more victories. This feeling didn't come because I was wrestling in the semi-finals of state. No, it came because I had beaten Wayne Love. I figured, if Matt Furey was good enough to beat Wayne Love, who was considered unbeatable, I had the skills to beat anybody I set my mind on beating. Anyone in the world

And so, when I walked onto the mat against Nekvinda I entered a new phase of personal power. Six minutes of my life, six minutes wrestling Wayne Love had steered the course of my life in a new direction. What would my life have been like if I had lost? Would I remain a doubter, forever skeptical of my own talent against the best competition? Would I ever get another chance to convince myself that I could accomplish great things?

My match against Nekvinda was giving me more chances, more opportunities; one of which was to wrestle in the state finals. Another was to show that my previous victory wasn't a fluke. It was a chance to prove to myself, once again, that I could beat the best wrestlers the state of Iowa had to offer. And with the victory over Love chiseled in my memory bank, I could use it for the rest of my life as a success to build upon.

I began the match with Nekvinda with the same intensity I ended with against Love. He was about the same height as I was but his physical build was not as thick, so I used this information to convince myself that he was in for a thrashing.

I tore after him from the moment the opening whistle blew. We pushed, pummeled, and fought to control one another with our arms, and when I secured the inside biceps control I wanted, BAM, I exploded into him with my favorite move: the duck-under. It was a move I'd practiced relentlessly. It allowed me to sneak beneath my opponent's arms and cause him to lose balance. If executed perfectly, my opponent would fall to the ground before me. Nailing someone with this move made wrestling look and feel effortless. Why couldn't all moves work this way?

10,000 duck-unders.

That's how many times I'd practiced the duck-under over the last month, and it showed. I scored over and over in match after match, using this move so often you'd think the victim would see it coming and be able to stop it. But my opponents usually couldn't because the move seemed to come from out of nowhere.

In spite of my success with the duck-under, this was the first time I used it at the state meet. I didn't have a chance until now, but man, once I saw and felt the opening, I was gone in a flash. When I hit my duck-under against Nekvinda I was pumped with excitement. Just as in previous competition against lesser foes, the move worked with an effortlessness that felt magical. As if he was being pushed by an invisible force, Nekvinda fell to the ground like a meteor being dropped from above.

I instantly went to work, applying pressure on his arms from the top position, trying to turn him over for back points. But despite his average build, Nekvinda was highly skilled in the bottom position. He was deceptively strong and my efforts to crank him over proved futile.

I decided to release him, intentionally sacrificing one point for an escape. It was a tactic I learned from the wrestlers at The University of Iowa and it helped blow a typically close match wide open. Because I wanted to increase my lead by more than two points, I chose to keep Nekvinda on his feet, where I had an advantage. If I scored another takedown, I would be ahead 4-1. This was better than 2-0, and it was the lead I wanted to take into the second period.

I attacked him with my duck-under again. But unlike most opponents who don't catch on, Nekvinda did. He countered and almost took me down. I attacked again, he countered again. Each time I attacked he successfully thwarted my efforts.

There are percentages involved in everything in life, including wrestling. Based on the Law of Averages, I believed I would eventually get him again if I stayed aggressive and kept up the pressure. If I kept attacking, he would eventually miss his counter-attack. Or he'd stop me and get the takedown.

Instead of going for the same move over and over, I switched gears a bit. I mixed it up by attempting a single-leg takedown, then a double-leg. Nekvinda stopped both moves easily – but then my opening for the duck-under came once again. Without forcing the move like I had in previous attempts, the move worked the way it is supposed to work. Nekvinda fell to the mat, one second before the buzzer signaled the end of the first period. I had the 4-1 lead I wanted. My confidence soared.

I won the referee's coin toss and chose the down position to start the second period. With a quick stand-up leading to an escape, I'd be up 5-1, and with another takedown it would be 7-1. This was the plan I envisioned - and if it worked I was assured victory, provided I didn't make stupid mistakes and kept up the relentless pressure, hammering away on him, never letting up until the final buzzer sounded.

Then reality hit my plans with a loud WHACK.

Nekvinda may not have been good on his feet, but he was great once he got the top position. From this position he pinned most of his opponents... and 20 seconds into the second period, he wrapped my head, right arm and leg up in a vice-like cradle. He rolled me onto my back. I looked out of the corner of my eye and saw the referee waving his hand back and forth, counting out loud, "One, two, three, four, five."

Damnit. I'm in a cradle. Get off your back.

Nekvinda held the cradle while the referee put up three fingers and said, "Three point near fall, green (Nekvinda)."

The score was now tied, 4-4.

But the present score didn't matter much if I got pinned, which would end the match. And I was very, very very close to having both shoulder blades flattened. I fought like a beast, desperately trying to break out of Nekvinda's cradle. Sweat poured off my brow. Trying to break his grip was like trying to pull yourself out of quick sand. I didn't know if I would ever free myself, but I kept kicking and struggling nonetheless, all the while fighting to keep space between my left shoulder blade and the mat.

After 15-20 seconds, I found the weak link in his grip. I clamped onto his fingers and squeezed them like my hand was a pair of pliers. His grip weakened. I ripped his hands apart. When I scrambled to my stomach, my whole body was drenched in sweat and for the first time during the tournament, I felt a bit fatigued. Nothing takes the gas out of a well-conditioned wrestler faster than being hit with a move that forces you to fight off your back. This is called "the element of surprise."

My plan was now crushed. And with the pressure Nekvinda was applying I felt like I might be on my stomach for the rest of the period. Where did the easy escape and takedown I planned on go? I glanced at the scoreboard. My three-point lead was gone and the clock was not going to stop so I could rest.

Nekvinda started to pound on my arms and neck like a gladiator wielding a sword. Every time I turned my head he smacked me across the face with his forearm and tried to wrap my head, arm and leg up in another cradle. He had more cradles, from more positions, than I'd ever seen or experienced before. I couldn't move without being in danger of getting rolled into the fetal position again, with my shoulders flattening toward the mat. But I learned a lesson from my first near-fatal mistake and was determined to not let it happen again.

I fought off my stomach and moved into a tripod position with my feet and hands planted on the mat and my butt arched high in the air. Nekvinda reached over my shoulder, trying for another cradle. I grabbed the palm of his hand, preventing him from locking his hands. He pushed me forward and I used the momentum to come to my feet. I spun around quickly, throwing him off balance, and broke free to earn my one-point escape. I was ahead once again, 5-4. Now I could work the strategy I formed when the period began.

From now on I'm keeping you on your feet. You're a dead man, Nekvinda.

I took my right hand and started to pound on the back of his head and neck, trying to set him up for more takedowns, but also trying to psychologically and physically defeat him. If I could break him mentally the physical part of the match would be much easier.

Nekvinda wouldn't give up though. He charged forward, pressuring me, looking for an opening to toss me to my back. I held his right arm with my left, stuck my head in his chest to create space in his defense, then threw his arm backward like I was reaching for a gun in its holster. He lost balance and fell to the mat once again.

Another duck-under scored. YES!!!

I held Nekvinda down for ten seconds and the buzzer went off, signaling the end of the second period. I led 7-4.

I knew I needed to build on my three-point lead if I wanted to win the match. I remembered how quickly Nekvinda could score on me with his cradle, so I gave up an intentional escape point when the third period began, making the score 7-5.

He charged toward me once again and I popped his elbows up and out of the way. My right foot penetrated the space between his legs and my hands grabbed his legs. I lifted him up in the air, twisted his body to the side and held him on the mat. Takedown Furey. I led 9-5.

Nekvinda was now getting tired and I was getting my second wind. He gasped for air. When I saw this I knew he was almost done psychologically. All I had to do was continue to make life uncomfortable for him; to never let up or let him relax. I wasn't going to stop moving for one second. I would push through the tiredness. Fatigue would not make a coward of me. With a four-point lead and an opponent who was more fatigued than I was, I decided to see if I could get him on his back for more points. Maybe he was tired enough that I could pin him.

From the side of his body, I drove into him, collapsing his left arm to the side of his chest. His arm was weaker than it was earlier in the match and he was ripe for a chicken wing, my number one pinning combination. I laced my left arm inside of his, strapped my arm across his back and applied downward pressure. His shoulder was more flexible than most wrestlers so I needed more leverage. I drove his shoulder toward his ear to create additional torque. He winced in pain and turned onto his back. Yes, I was going to pin him.

Nekvinda bridged off his neck by pushing with his feet and arching his spine. He fought hard to get off his back, but he wasn't able to do so fast enough. The referee awarded me two points for a near-fall. I was in absolute command, 11-5.

One minute remained in the match. I continued to look for ways to turn Nekvinda to his back. But his body was elusive and his shoulders were too loose for me to wrap him up into another tight pinning combination. So I laced my left leg inside of his and started to pry on his neck, using my forearm as a lever. Nekvinda quickly spun his body in a circle, forcing me to lose balance, then, with 25 seconds remaining, he reversed me, making the score 11-7.

He grabbed my arm and leg again and started rolling me up into another cradle. I strained with reckless abandon, almost crying out loud for help. He groaned and yelled, giving one final burst to turn me over so he could pin me. Both of us collapsed in exhaustion when the final buzzer sounded.

I won the match 11-7. What a fight it was. Both of us paid a heavy price for this battle. We would leave the mat with nothing left.

Normally I would run off the mat, filled with excitement, but I had used all my power to win this bout, making sure I was in the finals. Walking to my corner was all I could muster.

Coach Greenfield met me in the corner, shook my hand and said, "Awesome job, Matt. Tomorrow you go for all the marbles. Just watch out for the cradle next time. That's about all this guy had."

I nodded in agreement, but my body was still shaking with the fear of what could have happened from Nekvinda's one move. "All this guy had" was almost too much for me.

Greenfield's wife, Marilyn, ran up and hugged me after I stepped off the mat, then said, "Matt, you looked tired out there. That was the first time I have ever seen you tired. But you kept moving and I thought, 'Maybe he'll catch his second wind.' Then, toward the end of the second period, when you were on your feet, your energy came back. But look at you now. You're soaked."

I nodded again in agreement. All I wanted to do was sit and rest, but at the same time, feelings of enthusiasm and excitement were growing inside of me, and I couldn't relax. Especially when my parents came down to offer their praises. Mom led the way and, this time, she not only hugged me, she kissed me on the cheek.

"Matt, we're so happy for you," she exclaimed. "You did it. You'll be wrestling in the state finals tomorrow night. This is a dream come true."

"Congratulations, son," my dad interjected. "That was one exciting match."

"Thanks," I said, wiping the sweat that continued to beat from my brow.

"Now Matt," my father continued, "I noticed that Nekvinda wrapped you up in a cradle. I kept looking to see if your shoulder was down, if you were pinned – and I'll say, your shoulder didn't look like it was flat, but it was pretty darn close."

"It was too close," I said.

"Now, I don't know much about wrestling, but I'm just curious. It looked like you just gave him that cradle. I've never seen that happen to you before. What were you doing to give him an advantage over you like that?"

"Jim," my mom interrupted. "Let Matt rest. He's had enough for the day."

Coach Greenfield, who was still standing next to me, handed me a towel and said, "Matt, we've got weigh-ins now. This will be the last one of your high school career. How do you think your weight is?"

"After a match like this, I don't think I'll have any problem," I said confidently. "But let's go check to make sure."

We walked back to the same locker room I weighed in at two days earlier, when I was a nobody, a nothing, a little guy from a little town in Iowa. The locker room was a different place now and I was a different person. Only a fraction of the wrestlers who weighed in before the tournament began were still competing for the state title. I was one of them.

Wayne Love was in the locker room, too. He was running around in plastic sweats again with his jump rope in hand. He had a few pounds of water weight to drop. I didn't feel like I had any more water weight left in my body. That's how dehydrated I was.

"Step on the scale if you think you're ready to weigh-in," the referee said.

"I'm ready," I said, stripping off my clothes.

"Aren't you Furey, from Carroll Kuemper?" the referee said.

"I am," I replied.

"You're the guy who beat Wayne Love this afternoon, huh?"

"That's right."

"And you won again tonight?"

"That's right."

"Congratulations. Now, let's see what the scale says." I stepped on and planted both feet in the middle.

"Turn around please," the referee commanded. I turned and listened to the clang of the scale being adjusted.

"Step off please. You made it," the referee said.

"What was my exact weight?" I asked.

"You were 166.5 pounds. With a five-pound weight allowance that makes you five and a half pounds underweight. Not bad, huh?"

"Not bad at all," I said. "I need something to drink and fast."

Coach Greenfield handed me two quarts of room temperature Gatorade. I devoured both of them within a minute. The fluid was such a shock to my body that I started to sweat all over again. As the perspiration dripped from every pore of my body, I looked at him and said, "Can we go eat now? I'm famished."

"In a little while," he said. "In a little while. Be patient. We need to wait and see who you'll wrestle in the finals tomorrow night."

Ten

My final high school wrestling match. I never thought about it until after I won my semi-final bout. The thought made me reflect about when my career began, and how far I had progressed. My family, each member, in respectable as well as lamentable ways, had contributed to my success, whether they or I were willing to recognize it.

My older brothers, for example, could claim credit for beginning my career, not only from the beatings they inflicted on me at home, but by enrolling me in a grade school wrestling program at the high school I attended.

I was in third grade and was only eight years old. The wrestling coach at the high school at the time, Mr. Donnelly, wanted to have athletes who were knowledgeable about wrestling when they started with him as freshmen, so he began what was called the Kuemper Future Wrestler's Clinic.

The clinic, which only lasted a week, started at four o'clock each afternoon and finished at six in the evening. It ran from Monday through Friday and two days later, on a Sunday afternoon, a tournament was held to see who might be a good wrestling prospect in a few years.

Every kid who went to the clinic showed up for the Sunday tournament. We were placed into a bracket of eight, according to our age and weight. Ribbons were awarded to the top three people in each category.

The tourney started at noon, and I remember two of my older brothers driving me up to the high school to watch me compete. They prepared me for my matches with reverse psychology.

One started off by saying, "Matt, you're a lousy wrestler, aren't you? I'll bet you get the shit kicked out of you this afternoon. I can't wait to see you rolling around on the mat, fighting off your back. You'll probably cry the same way you do at home. 'Leave me alone. Ouch, leave me alone.'"

"Yeah, and if you do, I'm going to call you "LOSER" for the rest of your life," the other brother said.

This was my first motivational talk before a match. Upon hearing it I decided to make sure the opposite of what they said took place.

When the tournament was over, and I had soundly thumped all three of my opponents, winning a first-place ribbon, what could they say? Funny thing is they were happy for me, but not wanting to show it, were as crass as they were before the tournament began.

In case you don't know it, I'll tell it to you now. The Irish have trouble expressing true feelings without sarcasm, and my brothers are no exception.

"Did you see Matt, today?" one brother said, knowing I was right there listening to every word.

"Yeah, I saw him," said the other brother, laughing to himself and taking a long drag on his cigarette.

"Did you hear him grunting out there?"

"Uh, uh, uh. Grunting like an animal. Every time Matt tackled his opponent, you could hear him go UNGGGHHH."

My brothers laughed so hard their insides shook. They were funny, and even though I knew I would get another beating from at least one of them within the next day or two, they were my brothers and I liked them, even when it was tough to do so.

*   *   *   *   *

My parents named most of the kids after people mentioned in the Bible, but if the Bible lacked the names my parents liked, they used Irish saints' names and these sufficed. Actually, the Irish saints' names were preferred. And if there was any doubt that the Irishmen we were named after were in fact saints, my mom always pulled out each particular saint's biography and read his life story to us.

My middle name is John and combined with the first name of Matthew, I am the only one in the family with two names coming straight out of the gospels. My mother told me that she wanted to name me Emmett, but she came to her senses when the delivering doctor spanked my ass, making me cry for the first time. I always hated being called Matthew and made it clear to everyone from the time I was ten, that Matthew was not the name of a wrestler. Matt was.

When I talked with Coach Greenfield one day about the names of tough wrestlers, he told me, "You can't think of a better name for a wrestler than Matt Furey. It's like something straight out of Hollywood. It's like comic book character perfect. Matt Furey. Fury on the mat. It's classic."

My father's name is Edmund, but he went by Jim for reasons that don't even need to be explained. I found out his real name when I was a freshman and used to take delight in finding a way to "rib" him. Whenever we had Parent's Night for a home wrestling meet, a night in which each wrestler's parents were introduced, I made sure that the slip of paper I filled out and gave to the athletic director always read, "Edmund Furey." And so, on Parent's Night, when I walked into the gym with my parents behind me, the announcer would say, "Matt Furey, the son of Mr. and Mrs. Edmund Furey." My father would implode and mutter loud enough for me to hear, "Now why in the hell do they always introduce me that way?"

He never found out why.

My father was, in many ways, a strict disciplinarian. When I lived in the same abode with him, most of my time was spent in my room, but not by choice – by edict. My dad could not stand to hear any ruckus when he was reading,

During my sophomore year with my dad, at parent's night.

so his most-used method of dealing with me was to say, "Go to your room." In many ways my room felt like a prison – and this was yet another reason why I found so much freedom in wrestling rooms.

The ultimate example of how my father dealt with me under trying circumstances took place between the summer of my sophomore and junior year in high school. One day, when I realized I left my bicycle over at my good friend, Steve Nurse's house, I asked my father if I could use his car to pick it up. He told me no. I became enraged because he never let me use his car, despite the fact that I already had my license for almost a year.

"I HATE YOU, MAN" I yelled.

My father didn't say a word in reply. He simply got in his car and drove away with a painful frown etched on his face.

Later on that evening my sister Sheila found me sitting with Steve at a baseball game, watching the two high schools in the city competing against each other. She ran up to me with a worried expression and said, "Matt, you need to come home right now. You're in big trouble."

"Trouble from what?" I questioned. "I'm watching the ball game. Leave me alone."

With increased theatrics she repeated her message. "Matt, I said NOW. You're in BIG, BIG trouble."

I stood up, looked at Steve and said, "I'll see you later."

About a minute after I walked through the front door of our house and sat down, there was a knock on the door. My sister and I were the only people in the house. She answered. Standing on our porch, was a tall man, dressed in a sheriff's uniform. In fact, it WAS the sheriff? What the hell did he want me for?

"I'm looking for Matt Furey," he said.

I walked to the front door. The sheriff held up a document. "Are you Matt Furey?" he asked.

"I am," I said.

"This is a summons for you to appear in court on July 5th, at 10 a.m. You are being sued by Mr. James Furey."

What? Is this a joke?

It was the strangest thing I ever heard, but the sheriff and my sister didn't act like it was a joke. I was being sued by my own father. I was told that in this trial it would be determined whether or not I would be allowed to continue living in our house. Worst of all, the trial date fell on the same week that I would be attending a wrestling camp in Iowa City, at the University of Iowa, led by my idol, Dan Gable, whom I had planned on meeting for the first time.

I was on my best behavior for the next two weeks, and the wrestling camp was a half-month away. Then one morning, when I was feeling low, my mom told me, "Matt, you'll need to find yourself an attorney to represent you against your father. Why don't you go down and talk to Leighton Wederath and see if he can get a continuance for you on the trial. If he can get a continuance set up for you, you'll still be able to go to Iowa City for your wrestling camp."

The thought of calling Mr. Wederath was embarrassing, but going to Iowa City to be coached by Dan Gable was more important to me than protecting my emotions, so I made the call and a meeting was set.

When I have told people this story in the past, some have said they didn't think my father was really going to sue me. They thought he was merely using the sheriff and the legal system to improve my behavior, that no father would *really* sue his son.

These people don't know my father. They don't know that I was home when he threatened one of my brothers, telling him that if they didn't stop yelling and screaming he would have him arrested. He didn't believe my father and tested the threat, figuring it was a bluff. When the sheriff walked into our kitchen and handcuffed his hands behind his back, and hauled him off to the county jail for the weekend, he learned a valuable lesson that I never forget.

My father doesn't bluff.

*   *   *   *   *

Mr. Wederath's office was twice the size of my father's. And he was twice as big. He looked to be about 75 years old. His face was wrinkled, his belly was large and his chin hung halfway to his chest. He sat a step higher than myself when he was behind his desk, reclining comfortably in a dark brown executive's chair. I sat before him, feeling low and small.

"So, Mr. Furey, what can I do for you?" he said, resting his hands behind his head.

"Well, uh, my mother asked me to come see you about getting a continuance for the trial I have against my dad," I said.

"You have a trial against your father?" he asked.

"Yes, and it happens to be during the same week that I am supposed to be in Iowa City for a wrestling camp," I answered.

"What exactly is your father suing you for?"

I told him the story about how I got angry and shouted at him, and while I talked Mr. Wederath looked at me as if what he was hearing was the craziest method he had ever heard a father use to communicate with his son. He listened as I talked and when I was finished, he paused for about a minute and stared at me, as if he wanted me to continue. Then he sighed and said, "Okay, I'll see what I can do for you. I'll call the court house and see if we can move your trial forward a month. I'll call you if I encounter any problems. But I think it shouldn't be any trouble for me to get you the continuance you've requested."

"Thank you, thank you," I said, standing up to shake his hand.

"You're quite welcome," he said. "Take care of yourself now, you hear?"

"I will. I will," I repeated, then sprinted out of his office.

When I walked through the back door of our house my mother had her back to me, doing laundry. "Is that you, Matt?" she asked.

"Yeah, it's me," I said.

"Well, what did Leighton say?"

"He said he thought he could move the trial forward a month."

"Oh, praise the Lord. Now you can still go to your wrestling camp."

I learned my lesson. I never disrespected my father again. After the camp he and I had a long discussion in which I apologized and thanked him for all he'd done to help me. He accepted, gave me a hug and dropped the case against me.

Eleven

The wrestling camp in Iowa City was a master's lifetime of learning crammed into five days. Meeting Dan Gable was something I dreamt about for years, and despite the fact that many of the kids in the camp would never become champion wrestlers at Iowa, he gave us the same respect and attention his own team could expect.

Gable's build was unlike any other wrestler's I had ever seen. When you considered the fact that he was an Olympic champion who wrestled six matches in the 1972 games in Munich, without surrendering a point, you would think he had gargantuan muscles. But he didn't. His forearms were solid muscle but they looked about the same size as his upper arms. His thighs were muscular too, but didn't outshine his calves. And although his waist was as free of excess fat as a tightrope and his chest was like a sheet of steel, once again, neither area looked substantially bigger than the other. Gable was built like an oak tree from top to bottom.

When he demonstrated moves it was obvious that he had the perfect build for the style of wrestling he embodied. There was nothing he couldn't do to an opponent, it seemed, regardless of how strong or quick he was. And when I watched him move I thought he was beyond human. He moved as naturally as an animal in the wild. When he showed a maneuver his entire body shifted at once; a symphony of synchronized movement. He didn't move an arm or a leg or one side of his body. He turned everything, and the muscle definition you couldn't see when he stood before you, popped out of his skin and vibrated.

Gable used me as a dummy when he demonstrated and when the skin on his forearms brushed against my face and neck it felt like needles poking me. The bones in his arms felt like jagged pieces of granite and although his body was always in a state of relaxed preparedness, when he moved, the thump of his forearms on my shoulders felt like a knockout punch.

Gable was the first fat-free human being I ever saw who was unquestionably healthy. And when I studied his facial features I found the trademark of a champion wrestler: cauliflower ears. I looked forward to the day when my ears would carry the same type of battle scar; the same tattoo of greatness.

Often times great athletes are described as having exceptionally high levels of energy; saying this about Gable would be the understatement of the century. Yes, Gable was full of energy but it wasn't a loud-mouth, bombastic type of energy. It was different. It was focused energy, channeled energy, energy directed toward a specific purpose.

Watching Gable move while listening to him talk was all you needed to witness to know you were dealing with a super human. The entire time he coached us he never stopped moving. When he talked his feet swept back and forth along the surface of the mat. He walked around in small semi-circles and continually shook his forearms and wrists as if he were trying to knock something off his skin. He looked toward you when he talked but his eyes were too intense and his personality too shy for him to really make lasting eye contact. When he spoke you knew he was talking to you, and you were inspired and intimidated at the same time. No one ever thought of questioning anything he said.

Gable was the god of wrestling.

When he showed how to execute a technique he entered another realm, a dimension none of us had ever been to before. His voice would fluctuate, beginning slowly and softly: "The first thing you want to do in this move, is establish some type of... CONTROL. I like to grab my opponent's arm, just above the elbow, and BITE down on it with my thumb and index finger."

The further along Gable got in the explanation, the louder and faster he talked. "Now put your head right here in his chest and lower your level so that you're in better position to SCORE."

When the move neared completion his voice wavered from high to low and as he finished talking his entire face looked like he was possessed. "Squat down a bit more and throw his arm back AS HARD AS YOU CAN. Drive into him and without stopping grab hold of his opposite leg and TAKE OFF LIKE A FREIGHT TRAIN."

Gable was obsessed. Not in the negative sense of the word. He was obsessed with what he loved: wrestling. The sport of Hercules captured his soul, his mind, his body, his entire life. He was the man I wanted to have coach me someday and I dedicated myself to being good enough to wrestle for him when my high school career was over.

This goal was quite a stretch for me at the time, because, aside from the all-freshmen tournament I won early on in high school, my wrestling record had never been anything worthy of the attention of a school like Iowa, who, at the time, had won six out of the last seven national titles. Being recruited to wrestle for Iowa would be the equivalent of being recruited to play football at Notre Dame when Knute Rockne or Ara Parseigian was the coach, or basketball at UCLA when John Wooden guided them to 10 titles in 12 years. But it was a dream I believed in and was willing to place bets on no matter how many defeats I suffered or how distant the achievement of the goal appeared.

My junior season was the first year that I posted a winning record on the mat. I wrestled at 155-pounds and finished with a 16-8 record. At the district tournament I lost my first match, which eliminated me as a contender for the state meet, while opponents whom I had defeated during the season, qualified.

Coach Greenfield knew how badly I wanted to be in Des Moines, wrestling in the state meet, and so, even after my season was finished, he took me to Coon Rapids, to work out with their team. Coon Rapids always had good wrestlers and several members on their team always qualified for the state meet. Although their high school was small, with a graduating class of no more than 50 students, they always had tough, mean wrestlers, most of whom were rugged, powerful farmers.

The wrestlers at Coon Rapids were an unusual group, compared to wrestlers I met from other high schools. This is quite a statement because it is difficult to find a group of athletes with more quirks, more bizarre habits, more uncanny desires, or more peculiarities than wrestlers. But the coach at Coon Rapids, Doug Greenlee, had a knack for taking these farm boys out of the fields, or out of the barn, whichever it was, and turning them into stars.

The best wrestler on his team during my junior year was Steve Cory, a 185-pounder, who became a two-time state champion. You would never forget Cory if you saw him. His build was powerful; every muscle on his body rippled;

including the muscles in his face. He had the look of an overgrown gymnast turned Olympic weight lifter. Yet, from what we were told, Cory never lifted a barbell or dumbbell to create his physique. He was 100% stud, 100% stallion, 100% workhorse. I suspected that he got his strength from bailing hay, which was much harder than lifting barbells, and an activity that a city boy like me could only speculate about. Cory never lifted a weight; I never bailed an ounce of hay.

When the state championships began that year, Coach Greenfield and I took a day off from school to go watch Cory win the title. As I sat in the stands I saw how he warmed up, how he prepared for his bouts, and when I witnessed what he did I told myself, *This is not that big a deal. This is not impossible. I can do this, too. Next year I'm going to be here. I'm going to do exactly what I see him doing. And like him, I'm going to win it all.*

Cory and I never competed against one another on the mat, because we were in different weight classes – but we did in the pool. Both of us competed on the swimming teams of our respective cities. He was a lousy swimmer and I was a champion; from the age of 13 through 17, I didn't lose a race in butterfly or individual medley and only lost once in freestyle.

Besides the fact that Steve Cory was a state champion wrestler and I was still in pursuit of my first title, we had other notable differences. The main one was in regard to which sport we loved. Although Cory was a champion wrestler, and received over 150 letters from colleges and universities around the country, his real love was football, and football was the only sport he elected to play in college. And although I had the talent in swimming to compete in college, and on scholarship, I had no desire to do so. The only thing I liked about swimming was the competition, and eventually that was not exciting to me either.

Everything about wrestling intrigued me the first day I engaged in the sport and although I didn't seem to have the natural ability to excel in it, at least not in the same way I did with swimming, I was committed to making up for my lack of skill with clarity of purpose and focused movement.

The first and last time Steve Cory and I spoke was when I was fifteen. Both of us were taking a break between races at a swimming meet between Carroll and Coon Rapids. During the break I glanced over at the Coon Rapids team, all of whom were sitting about fifteen feet away from me. Everyone on the team was stripped down to nothing but tight-fitting red Speedo suits with a white stripe on each side. When I looked at the team I saw a blonde-haired girl with shoulder-length hair sitting on a towel, staring toward me. Her face was magnetic. I couldn't stop looking back at her. Her cheekbones protruded enough to make the blueness of her eyes sparkle in the glow of the setting sun. Her perfectly shaped breasts poked against the fabric of her red suit, making it almost impossible for me to look away. *What an incredible body*, I thought, as I looked at her with a big smile stretched across my face.

The girl happened to be Cory's, and when he noticed who I was looking at, his lower teeth pushed forward, then his muscular jaw tightened. Before he could start beating his chest like Tarzan, he growled the words, "HEY, FUCKER," at me. It only took a second for me to recognize the trance I was in and pull myself out of it. I quickly changed my appreciative smile into a humble shrug of the shoulders, punctuated with the words, "Sorry, man."

Luckily Coon Rapids had other beautiful women for me to focus on. One was named Misty. She was two years younger than me, but man, you wouldn't have known it if you did a naked body scan. She had dark brown hair, soft olive skin and brown eyes that twinkled when she laughed. She wasn't a very good swimmer, either, but because she admired the way I swam, she always found an excuse to wander over to our team's sitting area, so we could talk.

"How do you think you'll do in your next race?" she questioned, the first time we talked.

"I think I'll win," I said nonchalantly.

"God, I hate you," she said. "You always win."

"That's not true," I said. "I lost a race three years ago."

"Three years ago? Oh, you poor baby. I feel so sorry for you."

"But you know, winning and losing doesn't mean anything anyway," I lied.

"Right, right. Then let's see you go out and lose the next race on purpose. Swallow some water half way through the race and stick your head out, gasping for air," she said.

"I'm afraid I can't do that," I said.

"See, I knew it. You're just like the guys are here in wrestling. They never lose," she said.

"I haven't reached that level yet in wrestling," I said. "But when I do, will you still hate me."

"I'll always hate you," she said, smiling.

Three seconds was about all I needed to fall in love with Misty. We got together many times the summer before my junior year for movie watching and roller skating, but because of the differences in our religion, her parents didn't allow me to keep seeing her. We never spoke again. But before the state meet, when Coach Greenfield took me to Coon Rapids to train, I hoped I would see her there. Never did.

I suspected she was in Des Moines that weekend. I couldn't help but wonder whether she saw my match with Wayne Love and if she did, what she thought about it.

Although Steve Cory graduated a year earlier, the Coon Rapids team, as predicted, was still tough as nails. Two of their wrestlers, Marty Davis and Kim Reis, both of whom were seniors, were in the finals, too. Along with me, that made three wrestlers from Carroll County in the finals.

Butterfly was my best stroke. I was undefeated for four-straight years.

Twelve

Coach Greenfield and I waited in the locker room after I weighed in, expecting to hear the results of the other 167-pound semi-final bout from one of the referees. The combatants were Fritz Stratton of Muscatine and Jeff Roman of Cedar Rapids, Jefferson – two guys I didn't know much about. I felt confident about having to face either man, despite my lack of knowledge about them. I had beaten the unbeatable man and who could be tougher than him?

My ankle didn't hurt me like it did a week ago, and I didn't feel a need to protect myself from injury, like I did in the finals of the district tournament. Tomorrow night would be my last high school match and I believed I would return home as a state champion.

I decided to take a shower while we waited to find out who my opponent would be. Several other competitors were already showering when I took my place beneath the water. When I saw the look on each person's face, I immediately knew who was victorious and who wasn't. Almost everyone had abrasions and cuts, and no one looked as fresh as they were when the tournament began. I was feeling bruised myself – my first experience of competitive wrestling at this level: it is a brutal sport that can leave the winner feeling as beaten up as the loser. But even so, the winners still had a certain glow, a look of contentment on their faces, while the losers usually looked forlorn, humiliated.

When I got out of the shower I toweled my wet skin dry. My muscles ached. I really needed the 24-hour rest we had before the finals. Coach Greenfield's voice was hoarse from yelling and when he came up to me to tell me the result of the other semi-final bout it was painful for him to speak.

"Roman lost," he whispered. "Tomorrow night you'll face Fritz Stratton of Muscatine. He won 8-6."

"Fritz Stratton, what do you know about him?" I asked.

"I don't know much about him but I'll ask around. All I know is that in the quarterfinals, Sturdevant of Fort Dodge, the guy you lost to in the district finals last week, was beating him most of the match, but in the third period he got tossed onto his back and lost, 9-4," said Greenfield.

"Nine to four," I said, trying to calculate how tough my match with Stratton would be.

"Don't think too much about it," Greenfield said. "Get dressed. Let's get something to eat."

When we walked out of the locker room my mom and dad were looking for us.

"Maaaatt. Maaaatt," my mom yelled, trying to get my attention. "I just got off the phone with Uncle Jack. I told him you'll be in the finals tomorrow night. He couldn't say anything. He just cried and cried. He's so proud of you. I called the boys, and everyone is so excited. Sheila is going to drive home tomorrow from Omaha so she can watch. And Mal is going to drive down from Minneapolis."

"That's good," I said.

"Did you hear who you'll have to rassle tomorrow night?" my father asked.

"Yeah, I did. Fritz Stratton. He's from Muscatine."

"Muscatine?" my dad barked. "They have rasslers in Muscatine?"

"They're not too bad," said Coach Greenfield. "I heard they have two guys in the finals."

"You'll do just fine," my mom said. "Don't worry. Put everything in God's hands and you'll win."

"I'm going to need all the help I can get," I said humbly. "He beat Sturdevant from Fort Dodge, in the quarterfinals, 9-4."

Thirteen

On Saturday morning the phone in our hotel room rang over and over with calls from family and friends, people who wanted to hear my voice one last time before I became "famous." They would be watching me on television in the evening, yelling and cheering from Carroll to Souix City as well as Omaha, Nebraska.

The first person I talked to was my Uncle Jack McGrath, from Omaha. Jack was my mother's brother and the only lifelong bachelor in the family. My mom told me he was close to marriage on a couple occasions, but he always changed his mind as the day of matrimony drew near. Jack was my favorite uncle, mostly because he was a renegade. If he were married, I doubt if he would have spent as much time with me, and he probably wouldn't have been the practical joker he was.

Jack was more than a few pounds overweight and whenever he saw me he told me tales of how he'd been working out at the local YMCA. Even though he wanted to feel like we had something in common when he said this, he didn't need to fabricate stories to win my approval.

Uncle Jack was probably the only person in Nebraska who hated the Cornhusker football team, and the happiest moments of his life took place whenever they lost. The first thing he would do was call his brother, Tom, who also lived in Omaha.

"What's doing?" he'd say to Uncle Tom, as if nothing important had taken place in the last month.

I never knew exactly what Uncle Tom said back to him, but I knew he was belly-aching about the game Nebraska lost, because Jack would smile at me while pretending to be sympathetic.

"Oh, that's too bad," Jack would say, winking at me. "Nebraska is such a great team."

Then as if Jack never watched the game, he'd ask what the score was and what happened to cause the loss. When he hung up the phone he'd look at me and laugh, saying, "You should have heard your Uncle Tom whining. A grown man balling like a little baby because his football team lost. You should have heard the pain in his voice when he told me the score. Hehehe. I hope they lose again next week. Wouldn't that be the greatest? He'll be so ashamed he'll probably quit wearing his red underwear on game days."

When I spoke with Uncle Jack in the morning, he wasn't the typical uncle I knew. Normally, when we talked, he would spend most of the conversation rehashing yesterday's news. He had a way of making anything someone in the family did, even ten years ago, that showed the slightest ignorance or stupidity, sound like it happened last week and was a hundred times worse than it was. He was a true Irishman, a man who could tell a tale so well it didn't matter whether it happened or not. True joy came from listening to him fabricate stories he eventually came to believe himself.

But today was different. Uncle Jack was different.

"Matt, what's doing?" he said, starting our conversation the same way he began all telephone chatter.

"I'm wrestling tonight in the state finals," I said.

"You are? When did that happen?"

"It happened Thursday and yesterday. Didn't mom tell you?"

"Oh, that's right. She did. Yeah, she did tell me."

"So tonight is the big night," I said.

"You must be really proud. I'm sure proud of you," he said, changing gears. "Congratulations, You've made me happy to say I'm your uncle."

"Thanks."

"Matt, when the tournament is over, make sure you come up to Omaha and visit me. I'll take you out to Angie's for a big steak."

"I will. I'm getting tired of the steaks mom cooks me at home every night. They're not bad, but nothing is as good as a steak at Angie's."

"That's the truth, isn't it?"

"It is," I said.

"Matt, I gotta go," said Uncle Jack, "but I just wanted to call and wish you the best. Alright?"

"Thanks a lot, Uncle Jack. I'll do my best."

"I'm sure you will. Now say hello to your mother for me."

At ten o'clock, a few minutes after talking to Uncle Jack, I received a call from our high school athletic director, Mr. Balk. This was the first time the two of us had ever talked. Although I had great respect for him as a coach and teacher, I never knew what he thought of me, or if he cared about my wrestling success.

My insecurity in talking to Mr. Balk evolved around an incident with an older brother, who was the first one in the Furey family to show my father that high school wrestling isn't the phony professional rasslin' he suspected it was.

My father didn't want to attend the matches because of his perception of what the sport involved, but with my mom's gentle coaxing, he agreed to go. It only took one evening for my dad to fall in love with wrestling, deeming it the greatest present day test of an athlete's mental and physical powers.

My brother had the talent to become a great wrestler. But he made one mistake when he was an athlete at Kuemper: he went drinking with his friends. They holed up in a barn a few miles outside of town and got caught. When Mr. Balk found out about the violation of the athletic code, he supposedly told my brother that he could "never compete in sports at Kuemper again." At least that's the story I heard.

My brother then transferred to another high school. Unfortunately, it didn't have wrestling, so the only other sport he participated in was football. He never wrestled again, except for the times before he went back to Omaha where he also lived and worked. He used to toss me around on our front lawn, and unlike my other brothers, never really knocked me around much.

The good thing to come of this story was that because of what happened to my brother, my fear of being thrown out of wrestling was so great I made sure I never touched a beer or anything else that violated the athletic code, whether I thought I could get away with it or not.

So when I spoke to Mr. Balk, thoughts about my brother were in the back of my mind, and I felt grateful for having the discipline to act the way athletes at our school were supposed to act.

Mr. Balk was the pensive type. Outside of the algebra classes he taught, he didn't say too much. He retired from coaching a few years before I started at Kuemper and besides teaching, he spent much of his spare time thinking of creative ways to improve the athletic programs at the school, which was no easy task.

I never knew what he thought of me as an athlete, but from the time I was a freshman, I wanted him to know that I was not another member of the herd of new heads enrolling in school; those who put in four years and departed without making a significant contribution. And so, when he started talking to me, I learned the unspoken thoughts he had about me.

"Matt, this is Dan Balk."

"Uh hello, Mr. Balk. How are you?" I said.

"Matt, I just wanted to call and wish you good luck in your match tonight," he said.

"Thank you, sir."

"You know Matt, you have done a tremendous job representing Kuemper High School and the entire city of Carroll. You have greatly contributed to the school through your wrestling achievements and I want you to know that everyone is proud of you."

"Thanks."

"I also want to tell you that regardless of what happens tonight, regardless of the outcome, win or lose, we're still going to be proud of you."

I paused for a moment, then said, "Uh, thank you, sir," once more.

"Matt, is Coach Greenfield there?" Mr. Balk said, changing the subject.

"Yes, he is," I said, passing the phone to my coach.

As I sat on the bed, looking at the blank television screen, I began to feel down. Although Mr. Balk truly meant the best for me, his words felt like they were letting me off the hook. I thought to myself that he didn't care if I won or lost. To him, I'd already accomplished enough. My entire career had been built around garnering respect and admiration for winning, and now it appeared I already had the adulation of others, regardless of my performance. I wished like hell he would have said, "Matt, we're looking forward to another victory tonight. You've got what it takes to win – now show the whole state what you're made of." A message like this would be inspiring, uplifting.

I'm also sure I would have felt better if he said nothing at all. Too much babbling before a match rattled my nerves. My mother was the only person who knew this truth about me. During my freshman and sophomore years, when I was leaving the house to board the bus for an out-of-town tournament, she would say, "Good luck, Matt."

I hated those words more than anything. "Wrestling isn't about luck, it's about skill," I would say, snapping at her.

By the time I was a junior she learned that it was best to not say anything to me, to leave me alone, and if anything was going to be said, it would be said by me. If I felt relaxed enough to speak, she would usually hear me say, "I'm going to bring home the gold today."

If she nodded back at me and quietly smiled, I did as predicted.

I was one of those athletes you motivated before a match by saying next-to-nothing.

Fourteen

"If you want to be a champion wrestler, you need to focus your mind on winning and never think about losing," Coach Greenfield told me after I suffered an embarrassing defeat during the middle of the season, dropping my record to a dismal 7-4.

"Today you weren't concentrating. You made mistakes you normally don't make and mistakes are mental. They begin inside your head, then you make them physically. You want to be so mentally prepared for each match that all you can think about are the moves you want to make and how you are going to counter your opponent."

After my loss I was so upset I couldn't stop searching my mind for a way to rev up the results I wanted to achieve. I wanted to be a state champion. I wanted to wrestle for Gable – and I had a 7-4 record. What a joke. There was absolutely no way I was ever going to achieve my goals.

Yet something inside me wouldn't give up the dream, no matter how badly my season was going. The next day I went to the school library again, checking out my favorite book, **The Legend of Dan Gable – The Wrestler** for the umpteenth time. I signed off on the card in the book with my trademark "XXX" – then grabbed a seat at a table and began to look for the answer to my dilemma.

I combed through the book like I was looking into a microscope to study nuclear power. After several minutes I came upon a passage that shook my spine. For years I swore that I read, "Spend more time on the mat than anyone else." But the actual words I read were as follows: "Three workouts a day – year round."

Six words. That was it. Along with my interpretation of them.

The secret I found in re-reading this book after my loss changed me forever. If I was going to rise above my defeats, if I was going to achieve my goals, it would be done by practicing my wrestling moves more than anyone else. Yes, the running, rope skipping, calisthenics, weights and so on helped me get where I was – but to go to the next level, I needed to be on the mat every single day, and not just once. I needed to be on the mat practicing nothing but wrestling moves, three times a day.

Once I figured this success formula out, I wasted no time. Each and every non-competition day for the remainder of the season, I got on the mat three times and relentlessly repeated the moves I wanted to be able to execute as easily as inhaling and exhaling. The results of putting this formula or **Law of Practice** into operation didn't just help me win 14-straight matches. The formula helped me knock off the unbeatable man and put me in the state finals. What a turnaround! Think of it, anything you aren't good at right now, you can become good at if you'll practice more than anyone else.

In less than twelve hours I wanted to be the epitome of concentration when I wrestled in the finals. I wanted to wrestle a flawless match using every technique I practiced on the mat, three times a day, for the past two months. But because I was having trouble focusing after the phone calls, I closed my eyes and tried to clear my mind.

I pictured what I wanted to have happen when I wrestled Fritz Stratton. When I could picture the moves I wanted to execute, I imagined how they felt in my body, how they felt when I performed them live. If I could see the images of the moves in my head, while simultaneously feeling the power of each explosive maneuver in my body, I knew I was mentally prepared for victory.

* * * * *

Concentration is a big part of any sport, but I think wrestling requires more than most. People who know wrestling say that it is 90% mental, but based on the best and worst experiences I have had on the mat, I don't agree. Mental is not really what wrestling is, although it is a sport that uses the mind, and to a large degree. But the mind isn't all that is required.

I explained this concept one day to Fr. Walding, a good friend of my parents, when he came to our house to visit. Like most priests, he always wore a black suit, buttoned to the top, with a white collar prominently displayed below his Adam's apple. His glasses usually hung lower on the left than the right and one of his upper front teeth was half-golden, half-white. A smile always rested on his face, except when he was praying,

On this particular day, my parents and I were sitting in the living room, talking with Fr. Walding after he finished eating a couple slices of my mom's homemade apple pie. Mom's apple pie was his favorite pastry and I didn't know how he managed to stay slimmer than most priests in my hometown, especially when he never exercised. Fr. Walding loved talking to me about wrestling and I was surprised the day he asked, "Matt, isn't wrestling about 90% concentration?"

"It is," I said. "But the concentration isn't always in your mind. Most of the time it's in your body."

"How do you mean?" he asked.

"Well, imagine that you were playing chess. When you play chess you play it with your eyes and after you have imagined the move you want to make, and have thought about the possible counter moves your opponent will make, you act. But wrestling is like playing chess with your body. Sure you concentrate with your mind, sure you want to see what you and your opponent are doing. But so much of the action is impossible to see. You have to FEEL it. And when you react, your reactions have to be an automatic reflex. You can't sit and ponder for awhile like you do in chess."

I stood up and took a wrestling stance to demonstrate further. "Let's suppose an opponent is behind me with his hands locked around my waist. I can see his hands but I can't see the rest of his body. He's playing chess with me. He's pushing or pulling me, and I have to react to whatever direction he tries to take me. I have to be able to sense what he is doing. How can I do that if I rely only on my sight?"

"I see," Fr. Walding said. "But how do you feel what he is doing?"

"First, I have to feel his movements internally, like they're my own. Second, I have to make my skin like one thousand pairs of eyes. And even more than that, I have to be able to sense what he is doing, even before he starts doing it. I even have to sense what he is thinking about doing. I know it probably sounds strange, but it's the truth. When I am wrestling at my best, I really can feel the intent of his movements beyond my skin. I can feel them inside my own body. I can feel his movements as if they are my movements, as if I am wrestling myself. As if my opponent's nervous system is wired to my nervous system. When I can feel my body and his body as if they are the same, I know

I'm in the zone. I know I'm wrestling at my best. So, when people say wrestling is 90% mental or that it is 90% concentration, they don't have the whole picture. They're only partly right. Wrestling is 90% internal. This includes the mind, what you can see and what you can feel, as well as the strategies and tactics that need to be used."

"Fascinating," said Fr. Walding.

Yes, wrestling is fascinating. And on the eve of the state finals, it is fascinating to almost everyone in the state of Iowa. Even the people who didn't watch wrestling and didn't care about it found it fascinating when the state finals began. People at my high school who had never watched me wrestle, would watch the state finals. Friends who went to every home match would be coming to see the action in person. Some of them would even be in the front row, screaming and hollering for me on the way to victory.

My biggest fans were three men. They were men who were six, seven and eight years older than me; men who saw in me the qualities they wished more athletes in my hometown had. They were former wrestlers, former football players and lifelong weight lifters. They were all-state in wrestling and football, and if there was a statewide competition in coon and deer hunting, as well as fishing, they would have been all-state in those events, too. These men helped mold me into the wrestler I am today and they expected, with my victory over Love, that I would come home the victor.

Russ Hoffman was the toughest, strongest and most daunting one of the three. He was a first team all-state noseguard for Kuemper in 1975 and attended college on a football scholarship. The others, Joe Clark and Tom Feldman, were phenoms in their own right as well.

We used to get together on a regular basis to train, and it was Russ who really needed all of us to be there. The reason was because when he trained he lifted more weight than we thought the bar could hold. On the bench press he warmed up with 275 pounds, and gradually moved the weight up until the bar started to bend. On a bad day he could hoist over 450 pounds off his chest and when he felt better, he loaded as much as 515 pounds, which he could press two or three times.

When Russ worked out he kept his eyes on me; eyes that looked into the deep recesses of your brain. Whenever he thought I wasn't training hard enough he made my training regimen more difficult.

One time, when I was riding the stationary bicycle, he noted that my arms were resting on the handle bars. This was unsatisfactory, so he brought me a pair of 25-pound dumbbells and told me to pump them while I pedaled. On other days he wrestled with me, showing me how I had a long way to go before I could whoop him. I thought I was getting closer to being able to score on him one day, because I was able to shoot in on his legs faster than he was reacting. But I made the mistake of telling him I was quicker than he was, and that the only way he could beat me was by waiting for me to attack. Until that day, he always wrestled a defensive style against me and when I grasped his legs he crushed me with his strength.

When I told Russ about my superior speed he nodded as if he agreed, but the next time we wrestled, he showed me how wrong I was. Instead of standing and waiting for me to move, he attacked with one double-leg after the other. Each time he attacked, he scored, and each time he did so with finesse and speed, not strength. After 10-straight takedowns, he stopped, looked at me and said, "That's all for me today. Now why don't you go out and run a few sprints. You seem quite slow."

He escorted me out to the track and had me run a series of 40-yard dashes, and at the end of each dash, he stood over me, his toes under my eyes, watching me do pushups. While I ran he kept yelling at me, "I'll bet Gable ran faster than that when he was in high school. I'll bet Gable won't let anyone on his team who is as slow as you are."

When the workout was over, he gave me a water break, then said, "Now, if you want to be in shape to win the state title, if you want to be good enough to wrestle at Iowa, you should be able to go right back out on the track and do the workout all over again."

I believed him and we returned to the track for more sprints and pushups. I respected Russ more than anyone in my hometown and without his encouragement I knew it would be difficult to succeed.

Joe Clark was a 6'4" push-up marathon man with chiseled pectoral muscles and washboard abs. I first met him when he came to watch me compete in a swimming meet. I was thirteen at the time and Joe had heard the word around town that this short, stocky guy named Furey could race through the water like a dolphin. After I won the butterfly event by more than half the pool's length, Joe yelled at me from outside the fence.

"Hey, little Furey. Come here."

"Yeah," I said, walking up to the fence.

"How the hell did you get thighs like that?" he questioned.

"Thighs like what?" I answered, unconscious of how I looked.

"You got the biggest thighs in the world," he added.

I was a little uncertain at first because I didn't know the guy, but when Joe told me he was friends with my older brothers, I let down my guard.

I asked him what I could do to get stronger.

"I do 1,000 pushups a day," Joe said.

"Really," I said. "If I do that many do you think it will help me?"

"Start out slowly," he said. "Don't do 1,000 right away. Do four sets of 25 each day, and when that's pretty easy for you, do four sets of 35, then four sets of 50."

I followed Joe's advice to the letter and within two months I was doing 500 pushups a day. After four months I reached 1,000. The most I ever did was 1,500 – and that was as far as I was willing to go. Mainly because there were so many other exercises for me to do.

Tom Feldman moved to Carroll when I was a junior in high school. He'd recently graduated from Buena Vista College in Storm Lake, Iowa, and because he could easily bench press over 300 pounds, I figured he must have been the strongest 142-pounder in the country. His body was one big solid slab of steel and on the days he worked out with me on the wrestling mat, I was helpless. He moved like a cheetah and hit like a Mac truck. The most he ever said after beating on me was, "Wrestling is mostly desire. The guys who win are the guys who want it the most." I would need a lot more desire, and a lot more skill before I could beat him.

At my high school my only close friend was Steve Nurse. He was the eighth of nine children and his parents are my godparents. The two of us were humor buddies, not workout buddies, and throughout the wrestling season, he helped keep my spirits high with his imitations of teachers and students who had the slightest peculiarities. He was also instrumental in helping my ears become cauliflowered, but not by wrestling with me.

In the summer of 1979, after I came home from the Iowa wrestling camp, I told Steve about Dan Gable's cauliflower ear, and how it's considered the trademark of a champion wrestler. "I want to have a cauliflower ear, too," I said.

"Maybe you need some professional help," he quipped.

"Maybe I need to wrestle in practice without a headgear," I replied.

"That'll help," he said.

When wrestling season began my junior year I left my headgear in my locker. After six weeks of rough contact my right ear began to swell, filling up with blood.

"Man it hurts," I told him one day when we were sitting in class. "It feels like water on the knee."

"Does this hurt?" he said, flicking his index finger against my ear.

"Ouch. Don't," I said.

"I'm only trying to help," he said. "You told me you wanted an ear like Gable's."

"Yeah, but I never knew it would hurt to have one," I said.

"How much does it hurt?" he said, flicking me again.

"Damnit, don't," I whined.

"Sorry, man. I'm only trying to help."

"Well you're not helping," I said.

"Does this help?" he repeated with another flick.

"Cut it out," I laughed, despite the pain.

"How bout this?" he continued.

Today, because of Steve's "help" my cauliflower ears are a reality I will live with forever. The soft, painful swelling I felt when he finger-flicked me eventually became a hardened numb compactness, resulting in an ear that is undoubtedly malformed.

Steve and the others would be watching when I strapped on my headgear, covering my ears for the final match of my high school career. All of them knew what I had put myself through to be in this fight. From the muscles on my body to the shape of my ears, they had done their best to make me into a champion.

Fifteen

I opened the door to our hotel room at eleven o'clock and found an envelope laying at my feet with my name on it. I opened it and pulled out a card.

Dear Matt,

We want you to know that no matter what happens tonight, we'll still love you.

Good luck.

For the second time in one hour, someone was telling me the opposite of what I wanted to hear. Another we-love-you-no-matter-what message. Another message to help me save face in case I lost. Did anyone expect me to win? If they did, I'll bet their messages would have been different.

What a waste my efforts seemed to be. I worked for four long years, training two and three times each day to become a state champion, and now people were telling me it didn't matter if I won or lost. Baloney. It mattered a lot. It totally mattered.

My goal was to win – not to lose. Not to win or lose. To win, that's it... all of it. Two messages in an hour telling me how much I am loved and respected regardless of whether or not I win – these messages couldn't be their honest feelings. I couldn't believe someone would have the same respect for me as a runner-up as they would have for me as a champion.

People love champions – they are the people we respect and remember the most. Didn't they believe what General Patton said about winning and losing to his troops during World War II? "Americans love a winner and won't tolerate a loser. The very thought of losing is shameful to Americans."

Maybe these people thought they were doing me a favor, lightening the load for me, taking the pressure off – just in case I failed. But then again, maybe these people said and wrote what they did in order to be respected and admired, too. Maybe they were afraid that after I won it all, I'd no longer need them, that I'd no longer care about them, that they'd be forgotten – and I would be the only one remembered.

Maybe because they lacked the wrestling skills I had, they were expressing themselves in the only way they knew. I'm sure they wouldn't have done what they did unless they really believed it would positively affect me. It's quite possible they saw their words as encouraging; exactly what they would want to hear if they were in my shoes.

Whatever their reasoning, they meant well. Everyone loves to think that his or her words played a vital role in helping someone else fulfill a goal.

Let it go, I told myself. *I don't have time to sit around being annoyed. There is a title to be won tonight.*

Sixteen

Except for the time I spent eating steak and eggs for lunch, the rest of the afternoon was for concentrated rest. Before going to sleep the previous evening, I visualized myself going home as the champ, and I was doing the same now. I would be physically and mentally ready for the finals. Three matches were behind me – one more remained, and when it was over, I would become the second state champion in my high school's history. The first was in 1963. It was 1981 now and the drought had gone on long enough.

My mother, father and brother, Tim, drove two hours to and from Carroll and Des Moines each day, and this evening they would be accompanied by my sister, Sheila.

Sheila would get a free pass into the sold-out auditorium by becoming a Kuemper wrestling cheerleader for the first time in her life. She had no doubt that I would win the title. She was so sure of my eventual victory that before she made the ride to Des Moines she decorated our front porch with streamers and ribbons, as well as a gigantic poster saying: "WELCOME HOME CHAMP!"

Sheila had more faith in me than I had in myself. My mother told me I was her role model. When she went running on the Creighton University campus, she would push herself to new limits of endurance, telling herself, "I'll bet Matt wouldn't stop at two miles. I'll bet he'd run at least five. And at a harder pace." It was good to have her there, watching me in the finals.

As a sophomore in high school, when I first read about Dan Gable's high school life, I found out how he dealt with NOT having a sister. I read about the fishing trip Dan went on in Wisconsin with his mother and father, the summer after winning his first state title. His older sister, Diane, who like my sister was his greatest fan, stayed at home – and in their home, tragedy struck. A man broke through the back door of the house, raped Diane, then stabbed her to death.

The Gable family was devastated; Dan was the only child remaining. He decided that someone needed to be strong, someone needed to hold the family together, someone needed to give the family something to be proud of – and that someone was himself.

Gable re-dedicated himself to becoming a champion wrestler, and tortured himself with unheard of sacrifices. Legend has it that he did much of it for his sister. When he exercised in his basement, a picture of Diane hung on the wall, and Dan talked to her as he trained. He imagined she was still with him as he told her how his wrestling career was coming along and what she could expect him to accomplish in the future. She could count on him becoming a state champion, then a national champion, then a world champion… and after that, an Olympic Champion.

When Gable lost to Larry Owings in his final collegiate match in 1970, he was in tears, but the tears were not only part of the agony he felt from his first defeat in 181 matches. What bothered him most was what he told his parents when they went to the locker room to console him.

"I let Diane down," he said.

181-straight victories before the loss, and all he could think about was, "I let Diane down." If only my sister could have a brother with such passion and love.

No one had ever seen Gable lose before and no one knew how he would take his defeat. But when the awards ceremony began, Dan Gable took his place on the second step of the victory stand. The wrestling world was in shock. So was Gable. And when his name was introduced as the national runner-up at 142 pounds, the crowd of over 13,000, stood up and roared like thunder. The ovation lasted for several minutes and when Vic Marcucci, the man presenting the medals, walked toward Gable and handed him his award, Gable's face, as well as Marcucci's, were pouring forth tears.

Throughout every gymnasium in the state of Iowa, the news spread as quickly as a lightning flash through the sky. Basketball games, if you can imagine it, were stopped so the crowd who had gathered to watch dribbling and shooting, could hear the news.

"Ladies and gentleman, we have an important announcement to make. Dan Gable of Iowa State University, formerly of Waterloo West High School, has just finished the final match of his collegiate wrestling career against Larry Owings of Washington."

The announcer paused before continuing, unable to believe what he had to say. The crowd anticipated the opposite of what they were to hear. "And the result of the match... Owings 13... Gable 11. Larry Owings has broken Dan Gable's 181-match winning streak."

The following day the newspaper headlines in Iowa proclaimed the news in bold letters across the top. In the **The Des Moines Register** the headline read:

GABLE LOSES! GABLE FAILS!

Some time later, in a speech Gable gave, he said the loss may have been a blessing. The loss would help him dedicate himself even more than he already had. The loss would strengthen his determination to win an Olympic Gold Medal.

Many years after Gable won the gold in Munich, he told those who were closest to him, "I could feel Diane's presence with me when I wrestled in Munich."

My sister's presence would be with me for my final bout in Des Moines and I asked God for a piece of the same spirit that resided in Gable's mind and body.

Give me the strength to beat Fritz Stratton.

Seventeen

At half past five, Coach Greenfield and I packed our suitcases and loaded them into the back of his orange Toyota Celica. We would be going home after the finals instead of staying another night like most other teams, who had a larger wrestling budget than my high school.

When we pulled away from the curb, making our final voyage to the auditorium, Coach Greenfield said, "After you get your ankle taped, get out on the mat and warm-up. And make sure you take a lot of time loosening up. You haven't moved much all day and you'll need more time than usual to get ready."

"That's right," I said. "I know what it's like wrestling in a match when you aren't loose, and it isn't fun."

"And stay focused when you warm up," he added.

"I will," I said.

"Coach Kane will be meeting us at the auditorium tonight, too," he added.

"That's good," I said, remembering the hours Coach Kane had spent with me in the wrestling room when I was a freshman. At the time he started coaching me, freshmen practiced in the morning, but when he saw my dedication to the sport, he encouraged me to join the varsity in practice after school as well. Coach Kane was built like a fire hydrant; stubby legs and arms and a chest shaped like a barrel. I was thrilled to know he would join us for the finals.

"At a quarter to seven we'll head back to the locker room to line up for the Grand March," Coach Greenfield added.

"The Grand March," I exclaimed. "I forgot all about that."

"It's one of the best parts of the state tournament," said Greenfield. "It's also known as the Parade of Champions. Each year, the top six finishers in each weight class can take pride in being part of the group who walks around the mats to begin the finals. When the crowd stands and applauds, you're going to feel some mighty big goose bumps."

"I have goose bumps just thinking about it," I said.

Marilyn Greenfield told my mom about the event on the first day of the state tournament, and my mom held an image in mind of me marching in the parade when I wrestled in each match; she prayed for me to be one of the top six men left in my weight class.

Her prayers were heard. They were answered. The answer was YES.

When I took the mat at 6:15 to go through my warm-up, I felt as if every eye in the stands was focused on me, even though it wasn't the case. My body tingled with excitement and a hot wave of energy moved up and down my spine. I moved around in my stance, reminding myself of the fundamental skills I would need to use in the finals.

Keep your elbows in. Don't reach. Lower your stance – bend your knees – keep your back straight... lead with your head. Stay relaxed... but be intense.

I pictured my favorite moves and as each one moved through my mind, I practiced it with my imaginary opponent. He was with me again and I could feel his arms pushing against mine. I recalled the name of each move I wanted to use. I practiced each move while silently reviewing its name:

Duck-under. Fireman's carry. Double-leg. Single-leg. Snap down. Arm drag. High crotch. Bear hug. Hip toss.

I was on fire as I drilled and I wished our match could take place right then and there, at that very moment. I felt as if I couldn't wait another second. I wanted Fritz Stratton right NOW.

Come on Stratton, I'm going to kick your butt. You're gonna go home to Muscatine the loser tonight. I'm the best. I'm the state champion. Take your best shot at me. Come on. I dare you.

A loud buzzer sounded and the announcer said, "CLEAR THE MATS.

ALL WRESTLERS PLEASE CLEAR THE MATS. THOSE WRESTLERS WHO HAVE PLACED IN THE TOP SIX IN EACH WEIGHT CLASS, PLEASE REPORT TO LOCKEROOM A."

"Let's go." Coach Greenfield said as he stood at the edge of the mat.

I followed him back to Locker Room A and looked for my place in line. The referees organized us by our respective weight classes and I found where I belonged when a familiar face looked at me. It was the face of Wayne Love. There were four other men standing in the same line with him when I joined them. I stood to the left of Love.

Please don't say anything to me, I thought.

After losing to me yesterday afternoon, Love bounced back and trounced all of his consolation-round opponents. He mopped the mats with them like he did the year before when he won the state title. His final bout was for third place and he beat his opponent, 11-3. If I hadn't won my semi-final bout last night, we would have had a rematch, so I was grateful as well as relieved to be in the finals. The results of our match still played in our minds. Especially his. But because I had another match to concentrate on and he was already finished, he had more time to reminisce than I did.

We stood a foot from each other but our thoughts were miles apart. Love rapidly chewed his gum and kept glancing at me from the corners of his eyes. I looked straight ahead as if I was standing at attention in boot camp.

He was wearing his blue Waterloo Central uniform with a pair of cowboy boots adorning his feet. I moved my head to the side and looked down at his boots and when I did so he spoke to me for the first time.

"How ya doin'?" he asked.

"Fine" I said, looking at him long enough to make eye contact, but not long enough to become friendly. I shyly looked around for something else to focus on.

"I say, it's been a long time since I lost," he said.

"Hmm?" I questioned, meeting his eyes once again.

"I say it's been a long time since I lost," he repeated, leaning toward me a bit.

"Oh," I said, unable to imagine what else to say.

I don't think it's a good idea to talk about our match, I thought.

Love must have had the same idea because he changed the subject.

"Where you going to school to wrestle next year?" he questioned.

"Iowa," I said, sticking with one-word answers.

"Really? Maaaan, you gotta be pretty damn good to wrestle at Iowa," he said.

"Yeah," I said.

"How old are you man?" he asked.

"Seventeen," I said.

"You play football, man?" he asked, while looking at the stumps I have for legs.

"Nope," I said.

The way Love and I communicated was how I communicated with anyone I didn't know very well. I was protecting myself the way my father had taught me. From the time I was 10 he told me, "Matt, you've got to make people work for their information. Never answer anything more than the question you're asked."

After another minute of small talk I started to enjoy the conversation with Wayne, but our talk ended as soon as the Parade of Champions began. I had more important business to take care of now. Fritz Stratton was on my mind.

Eighteen

15,000 people stood and applauded when all the place winners for the 1981 Iowa High School State Wrestling Tournament stepped onto the mats, representing more than a hundred schools.

98-pounds, the lightest weight in high school wrestling, led the way and the unlimited class anchored. We were from Ames, Des Moines, Davenport and Waterloo. We were from Fort Dodge, Webster City, Humboldt and Mason City. We were from Coon Rapids and we were from Carroll. We were muscular, lean, mean and proud. We were the elite athletes in each weight category.

Enter 98, 105 and 112 pounds.

Enter 119, 126, 132 and 138 pounds.

Enter 145, 155, 167 and 185 pounds.

And along with the unlimited class, those of us who remained were the true "heavyweights" of each weight division.

Three minutes – that was the length of our parade, and when we sat down in the stands, the auditorium of fans who cheered without restraint, now stood quietly to honor the country with the playing of our national anthem.

Throughout the singing, as I proudly stood looking out at the multitude, I thought, *Matt, you've done a pretty good job, haven't you? It wouldn't be too bad to say you took second in the state. You should be proud of yourself for coming as far as you've come. You've done better than anyone expected. It really doesn't matter whether you win or lose tonight. The journey to the finals is the most important thing, not the match itself.*

Much of this was true, but those were thoughts I could ponder when the match was over. They were not appropriate ideas to think about now, before a championship match. But I was thinking these thoughts and I couldn't help myself.

I sat in the stands after the parade and the longer I sat the more I started to relive the experience of the telephone call from the athletic director and the card I received an hour later. I was off the hook. I didn't have any pressure on me. I didn't need to strive anymore. Win or lose, I was a good guy, a respectable person.

For the first time in the tournament, I was more focused on a negative result than a positive one. I was thinking more about losing than winning. Inside my own mind a battle raged. Every thought contradicted the previous one and I hated it all.

Second in the state isn't bad.

Bullshit. Second sucks. You want to be number one.

Don't worry, everyone loves you, win or lose.

Damnit. I only want to win. Who cares what others think?

You want to be the champ. That's more important to you than anything else.

You're not going to win.

The hell I'm not.

You're going to lose.

Like hell I am.

On and on the battle continued. Championship bouts were taking place in front of me but the biggest fight was going on inside my own head. The noise in the auditorium was deafening yet even louder sounds raced through the movie screen behind my eyes. My head was beating faster than my heart. I was lost in a maze of thoughts that were harder to fight off than any opponent I had ever faced. The thoughts throbbed, they hurt, they felt like handcuffs, shackles and a ball-and-chain. I was a slave to them, and each negative image, no matter how repugnant, grew in strength.

Every person who told me I'd never make it was in the forefront of my head and the strong person inside of me, the one who could make himself powerful in the midst of chaos – he was nowhere to be found.

There would be no more trips to the hotel for quiet, undisturbed solitude. My final mental preparations would have to be conducted in the middle of a crowd and no one in this crowd was going to come up to me and help me straighten myself out. It would have to be done by me and me alone. Alone in an auditorium filled with people yelling, shouting, screaming – sometimes crying.

Where was my success mantra for the finals?

Take one match at a time seemed useless to me now. This was my final match. There weren't any more after this one.

I needed a new mantra, a new phrase to help me focus.

Nineteen

Marty Davis of Coon Rapids was on the mat at 112-pounds, going for his second state title. With 30 seconds remaining in the bout, he was losing 13-7, and his defeat looked inevitable. But Davis thought otherwise. He was a warrior who never gave up.

Both men were on their feet when Davis' opponent, Ben Kreese of Maxwell, attempted to score another takedown. Davis pancaked him to his back, scoring a two-point takedown. The referee starting counting back points and Davis quickly secured a three-point nearfall as he tried to pin Kreese. Everyone thought Davis would keep him down and continue to try and pin him. If he didn't score the fall, Davis would lose by one point, 13-12.

With 15 seconds remaining, Davis surprised the crowd when he let Kreese go, giving up an intentional escape point. Now he was down by two points. But Davis wouldn't quit. He snapped Kreese to his knees and drove into him. He thrust his hips and chest into Kreese like he was hammering through a block of ice. The opposition couldn't stop Davis' momentum. He landed on his back a second time and Davis scored five more points. It was the most spectacular come-from-behind I ever witnessed and it gave me a renewed feeling of optimism. Down by six points with thirty seconds to go, and the guy wins by three points, 17-14. WOW!

Before the state tournament began, Doug Greenlee, the Coon Rapids coach, summed up what can happen in competition at this level when he said, "Mysterious things happen at the state tournament." How true.

The completion of the 132-pound final was my queue to warm-up. This weight class was my father's favorite because of one wrestler: Joe Gibbons. He was the best high school wrestler my father ever saw, and tonight was Gibbon's historic moment. He could become the second wrestler in Iowa high school wrestling history to win four consecutive state titles.

Coming from a family of wrestlers, with older brothers, Jim and Tim previously winning state titles; Joe turned out to be the best high school competitor in the family.

He thrashed his opponent, Russ Graves of Webster City, in the finals, 13-0, making it look like winning a state title was about as difficult as opening and closing your eyes. When I watched the referee raise Gibbons' hand I thought, *Man, if Gibbons can win four state titles, I should be able to win at least one.*

Three more weight classes remained before I would take the mat and provided none of the matches went into overtime, eighteen more minutes of clock time were all that remained before it was Zero Time again.

The tension in the back corner of the auditorium, where I warmed-up, was thicker than an iceberg. Heat rose from the heads of fans who cheered from their seats. And my negative thoughts slowly disappeared as I stretched the tension out of my muscles. Movement had always changed my emotional state before and it was working again now, when I needed it most.

I noticed that my focus was not as deep as it had been before my first three matches, so I ran through my warmup ritual, trying to force the magic to return. Nothing felt right. Each move I made lacked the power I desired. I decided to breathe faster. By increasing my breathing rate, I could give myself a surge of adrenaline. I imagined that I was Dan Gable and I tried to imitate what I thought he would be doing to prepare for a state championship match.

My focus returned. My concentration moved from the things I feared and centered on what was important to me. The pace of my breathing gave me the rush of adrenaline I wanted and a surge of enthusiasm flowed through my body. My legs felt like steel and if I could have seen the inside of my body, my blood would have looked like boiling lava ready to burst out of a volcano. I was impatiently excited and I didn't want to wait another second before letting my passion burst. The feeling of eagerness, the feeling of readiness I felt when I warmed up before The Parade of Champions was back. I wanted Fritz Stratton NOW.

But I had to wait... and the time I spent waiting felt like an eternity. Yesterday, time moved so fast I couldn't keep up. Today, I couldn't speed time up if I wanted.

Twenty

When the announcement for the 167-pound title bout finally came, it shook my white halo headgear and rattled my eardrums. I swallowed hard and felt a thump in my solar plexus as I heard: "167 POUNDS. ON DECK MAT ONE. FRITZ STRATTON OF MUSCATINE VERSUS MATT FUREY OF CARROLL KUEMPER. STRATTON VERSUS FUREY, ON DECK MAT ONE. PLEASE REPORT."

I took off running toward the mat with Coach Greenfield. As I did so my mind was where I wanted it to be. I was positive. I was in control of the demons who were rattling my brain. They were in cages now and their voices were asleep.

I'm going for the gold. I'm going to bring home the gold. I'm going to win it all.

Fritz Stratton looked like a Bengal tiger as he pranced back and forth in front of the scorekeeper's table. He was my last foe and he was as hungry for victory as I was. His eyes were calloused and intense as he strode back and forth in his black hooded robe with gold trim.

MUSCATINE was written across his back and the number 10 boldly stood out on his right sleeve. From across the gym you could see a long procession of 19 yellow safety pins attached to the front of his robe. Each safety pin represented an opponent he had pinned during the year. I had only pinned nine opponents during the year. Without a doubt, Stratton was a dangerous adversary.

A large contingent of Stratton fans were sitting matside chanting his first name like he was a god. "FRITZ, FRITZ, FRITZ, FRITZ, FRITZ, FRITZ..."

My fans countered, "FUREY, FUREY, FUREY," while waving red handkerchiefs with the letter "K" on them. When I saw them waving their handkerchiefs and yelling my name I knew it was Zero Time; the time when years of preparation meet six minutes of opportunity.

My feet pushed off the ground as I walked in circles to gather energy. I felt strong, incredibly strong – strong enough to whoop anybody. My eyes darted back and forth like an agent in the Secret Service. With one glance I could scan every inch of Fritz' body and find the slightest detectable weakness. Trouble is, there were none. Fritz was solid. This was going to be a tough match.

The final seconds ticked off the 155-pound match before us. I took off my t-shirt, baring my naked chest to the crowd one last time. I pulled my singlet straps up and snapped my headgear. I was ready.

These are the last six minutes of your high school career. Go out a winner. Focus out there for three two-minute periods and go home a state champion. You don't want to spend the rest of your life saying, 'I wish I would have tried harder.' Give 110 percent out there and victory is yours.

Coach Greenfield shook my hand as if the strength of his entire body was in his palm. He slapped me on the back and said, "Do your best."

"I will," I said, then turned and sprinted to the inner circle where our match began. The referee handed the green anklet to me and gave the red one to Fritz. It was the first match in the tournament that I would wear the green anklet and I didn't like it one bit.

But who wears what color is not my decision, so all I could do was put the anklet on and force the idea that red is a lucky color out of my mind.

Fritz put his right foot forward. So did I.

"Shake hands," the referee said.

"Good luck," Stratton mumbled to me as we locked grips.

Good luck my ass. I'm going to pound you, boy.

The whistle blew and the quest for gold began.

Stratton attacked me with a single leg. He held my right leg with both of his hands. His arms wrapped like a coil around my knee, his head pushed against my chest as he pulled my leg off the mat. I bounced around on one foot, trying to keep my balance. He pulled my leg upward, all the way up to his chin. He changed his grip, moving his arms underneath my leg, elevating my leg even higher. I bounced and bounced off my left foot. He couldn't put me down. I was too flexible. But he was more ferocious than most opponents and he overcame my flexibility by ramming me forward – sprinting at my posted foot while my other leg was close to his ears. He kicked my posted foot out of the way, soccer-style, as if he was booting a game-winning field goal. I fell to the ground like a toppled tree. He landed on top of me and secured the first two points. Stratton led 2-0.

The man was strong. He wasn't graceful, but grace didn't matter to him because he found a way to get the job done; brute strength and power were his weapons.

My sister was sitting at the edge of the mat, wearing her red and gold cheerleading outfit. She cheered so loud her voice began to crack. "COME ON, MATT" she yelled. "YOU CAN DO IT. COME OOOOONNN."

I struggled underneath Stratton's powerful arms. He pried at my wrists and forearms; using his hands like they were an electric drill – forging through my defense. I kept my elbows in and protected myself. He would need kryptonite to weaken me further.

I don't care how strong you are Fritz, I'm going to beat you.

Fritz drove his hips into my side, trying to knock me flat on my stomach. I scrambled forward on my knees, keeping a solid base. And then I found a leak, a gap in his attack. I turned my body over – almost exposing my back, then lifting my hips to create more leverage – I forced the arm he had around my waist down toward the mat. He winced in agony. Stratton fell to his stomach as I scooted behind him. Now I was in control.

"Two point reversal, green. Two points, green," the referee yelled, putting his fingers in the air.

2-2.

I worked my left hand inside the bicep of Stratton's left arm and held him flat. "DRIVE HIM TO HIS BACK," Coach Greenfield yelled. "DRIVE, DRIVE, DRIVE."

Only a few seconds remained in the period. 3, 2, 1. The buzzer sounded. Our first two minutes were a draw.

In the closing seconds of the first period, I found Stratton's vulnerable area. He couldn't ride me. I figured I could reverse him again when he drove into me. So I hoped I would get to choose the starting position for the second period. If I won the flip, I would take the down position. I would then score again right away and take a commanding lead.

The referee flipped his coin in the air. It spun around on the ground like a top, then landed with the color green facing up. I chose the down position. I was ready to rock.

"YOU GOT HIM WHERE YOU WANT HIM," Coach Greenfield yelled through his cupped hands.

"GO MATT GO. GO MATT GO," my sister yelled along with the other cheerleaders.

I took the down position, keeping a one-foot distance between my knees and hands. "Top man get on," the referee said. Fritz knelt behind me, putting his left hand around my waist and his right hand on my right elbow.

"Ready?" the referee said through teeth that held his whistle; looking to make sure there wasn't a false start. He raised his right hand high in the air, held it in position, then dropped it while simultaneously blowing his whistle.

Fritz immediately switched sides on me and worked to break me down to my stomach. I sat out, turned my body to the left and pushed into a tripod position. But as soon as I formed the tripod, Stratton slapped a cradle on me.

Damnit. Someone scouted me in the semifinals against Nekvinda. They saw him almost pin me in a cradle. Now Stratton was applying the same pinning combination on me.

What a sucker I was. I kicked, grunted, and worked on Stratton's hands, trying to pry them apart. He lifted my rolled up body onto his chest and hips and turned me to my back. The referee waved his arm along the surface of the mat, counting the seconds with each movement of his hand.

Stratton's grip was tight but my legs were stronger. I kicked his hands apart. The referee only counted four seconds. I avoided a three-point near fall by one second. Two of the referee's fingers pointed up in the air. He showed them to the scorekeepers and said, "Two point near fall, red."

Stratton led 4-2.

Pick up the pace. These are the last few minutes of your high school career.

I scrambled for better position, trying to get to my feet. But I couldn't get away. Stratton applied more pressure, and was careful not to make the same mistake he made toward the end of the first period. He stayed glued to me like a coat of paint, refusing to let go.

I got to my feet. He locked his arms around my waist, popped his hips into my side and tossed me back to the mat. With determination I pushed to my feet again – he locked his hands around my waist to prevent my escape. I knew I needed a second move from the feet to stop him from throwing me down again. His chin rested against my back. I directed my next inhale into my shoulders and rapidly whipped my upper back from left to right. My shoulders brushed against his jaw, making it pop. He couldn't hold on.

"One point, green. We have an escape for green. One point," the referee said.

I spun around and attacked Stratton with a double leg. It was too late. The buzzer hummed, signaling the end of the second period. The referee grabbed us to stop the action.

Stratton still led 4-3.

Two minutes remained. Two minutes that had to be more than II0-percent. I still had a chance to leave the state tournament as the I67-pound champion.

Stratton took the down position to begin the final round. I got on top and the referee blew his whistle. I lunged forward and Stratton turned away from my force. Before three seconds ticked off the clock he had a reversal.

6-3, Stratton.

"MATT YOU'VE GOT TO GET AWAY. YOU'VE GOT TO GET UP," screamed Coach Greenfield.

"YOU'RE THE BEST. COME ON, MATT. YOU CAN BEAT HIM." my sister yelled.

But I couldn't hear them anymore. The crowd was so loud I couldn't even hear the referee. All I could hear was the voice inside my head urging me on to victory.

You've got to do more, Matt. Get to your feet. Get away from him and take him down.

What a predicament I now had myself in. I had to get this hulkster off my back and I had to do it quickly.

1:00 remained in the match. The final 60 seconds of my career.

I exploded to my feet, pushed my back into Stratton's stomach and reached down, hoping to find a leg to grab onto. Stratton threw me back to the mat. But when I landed I kept moving and Stratton wasn't in position to stop my next move. I reversed him with the same maneuver that worked earlier.

"Two point reversal, green. Two points green," the referee barked.

6-5, Stratton. Furey closing fast.

The crowd noise grew louder with each tick of the clock. I couldn't hear anything anymore. Only my inner voice.

Score, Matt, score. Now. Do it now.

Stratton collapsed onto his stomach. He was exhausted with very little left in him. He laid on his belly, refusing to move. The referee caught his stalling tactic and immediately warned him. I was gaining momentum. I barred him up with the same chicken wing I'd turned Nekvinda with in the semifinals. But the sweat on Stratton's back weakened my force and my arm slipped out.

I applied the pressure again, barring him up a second time. This time the hold was tight. This time there was no escape.

0:35 remained on the clock.

I had to score and FAST. I cranked on Stratton's arm hard enough to snap it. I drove his head into the mat, raised his shoulder up a bit and directed it toward his ear. Now I would punish him. I would make him scream all the way to his back.

Stratton yelped in agony, ready to succumb to the pressure, ready to turn to his back. Victory was mine. His left hip came off the mat and his ribs were spreading further apart. I was merciless.

Cry all you want Stratton, you're going over.

But just before he would flop onto his back, my arm slipped against the profuse sweat coating our boiling skin.

0:21 remained.

I looked at Coach Greenfield for advice.

"LET HIM GO, MATT. LET HIM GO AND TAKE HIM DOWN. TIE IT UP AND BEAT HIM IN OVERTIME," he yelled.

I let Stratton go, giving him an escape point, but instead of immediately turning around to face me, he kneeled on the mat and wasted a few more seconds.

0:17 left.

7-5, Stratton.

I ran around him so he could see my face. I charged at him, but before I could get in position to score on him and tie the match, he leaped toward my exposed right leg and grabbed on. He held on like a leech sucking the blood out of me. I looked at the referee and pointed at Stratton, exposing his stalling tactic. The referee nodded, blew his whistle to stop the match and called a stalemate. No points were awarded.

The referee put both of us back on our feet, where we faced each other in the neutral position, just like when the bout began five minutes and fifty-five seconds ago.

0:05 remained. Could I pull off a miracle, a Marty Davis? Could I score some big points fast?

The whistle blew. The crowd stood up.

15,000 people were watching from above. Most of Iowa was watching on television.

Battling Fritz Stratton in the State finals.

Twenty-one

The finish was not pretty. It was not poetic. It wasn't miraculous. It wasn't anything I wanted. And the thought of it all can still make me cry, even 29 years after the fact, if I let it.

That whistle… I can still hear it today. It still rattles my brain and unsettles my nerves. It makes me want to move with the force and speed of a cheetah. It makes me want to do anything other than what I did in those five remaining seconds. It makes me want another chance. Every once in a while it wakes me in the middle of the night, and when my eyes open I look into the darkness of my bedroom and see the bright lights of the auditorium. I hear the voices I couldn't hear before – I see the final movements of our state championship match. And I hear the bleep from the referee's whistle again.

When I rub my eyes to convince myself that it's all just a dream, I see and feel the sweat bubbling on my skin. My body is drenched with sweat and as I wipe it off, my mind is thousands of miles away; it is still in Des Moines.

I don't like to think about what happened in those final five seconds but, for some odd reason, my unconscious mind still begs for an explanation, a chance to see it all again, a chance to recreate the whole scene – and then it all comes back to me when I sleep.

When I think about those five final ticks of the clock… they move sooooo slowly. I can't imagine the true quickness of those ticks because they were the slowest ticks a clock ever made in my life. Those ticks live with me forever. They are unforgettable. They are my history. And they'll never go away so I've learned to live with them and learn from them.

When I first began my high school wrestling career I couldn't wait to place the newspaper clippings about my victories in a scrap book. One day my mother noticed that the only clippings I kept were the ones in which I was victorious. She didn't approve of this.

"Matt, you need to be honest with yourself," she said. "You need to tell the whole truth. Life is full of good moments and it is full of not so good moments. You don't just look at the good things you've accomplished in life and pretend that you've never had a loss, never suffered, never had difficult moments. Look at everything. You will learn just as much, if not more, from your defeats, than you ever will your victories."

I never forgot my mother's lesson and as much as I'd like to bury those career-ending ticks, as much as I'd like to throw out the truth, I cannot. I must be honest and talk about the seconds that visit me in dreams. I must finish my story.

0:05 remained.

Stratton's face was crimson red. My hair was completely sopped in sweat. His forearms were shaking uncontrollably, filled with pain from the chicken wing maneuver I tried to turn him to his back with. My legs were trembling, barely able to hold me up – and I needed them to do much more than that.

When the referee blew his whistle Stratton and I moved toward each other. I reached up to snap his head, setting him up for the fireman's carry I successfully envisioned. But as soon as I moved my hand to snap his head he long-jumped underneath me, grabbed onto my right ankle and held on until the final buzzer sounded.

I couldn't blame Stratton for doing this. But damnit, I was angry about it. Angry because his last second move kept me from fulfilling my dream. His goal was achieved. He would go back to Muscatine as a state champion. I would go home forgotten. I was nothing but another state runner-up. No one knows and no one cares about the person who comes in second.

I slowly, dreadfully unsnapped my headgear and walked to the center of the mat for the final handshake of my high school career. As our palms met the referee grabbed both of our wrists and raised Stratton's right arm high in the air.

My wrist remained at my side. I lost. I fell short of my goal. Two points short. There was no glory in this. Winning was all I wanted. Even if people loved and respected me for my efforts, I could not feel love and respect for myself when I lost.

General Patton's words rung in my ears once again, as if he was standing right before me. "Americans love a winner – and will not tolerate a loser. The very thought of losing is shameful to Americans."

I felt ashamed. Defeat, when it is so close to victory, is insufferable.

Twenty-two

My head hung close to my chest as I walked off the mat. Coach Greenfield met me in the corner, put his hand on my shoulder and said, "It's alright, Matt. You gave it your best shot."

No I didn't.

Seconds later, the head coach from Fort Dodge High, who was preparing his 185-pound wrestler for the finals rushed up to me and tried to soothe my sadness. Putting his hand out to shake mine he said, "Matt, congratulations on an outstanding career."

Outstanding? How could my career be outstanding? I Lost. There is nothing outstanding about losing. There is no possible benefit in losing. I wanted to go to Iowa. I wanted to wrestle for Gable. Gable only wants champions on his team.

I tried to run off the floor of the auditorium but my sister stopped me. She was standing before me, crying. Her freckled hands covered her face as she sobbed. "I'm sorry," I said, "I didn't prove myself to be a champion tonight."

"You did prove it," she said. "You wrestled the best match of your life. Sure, the final score says you didn't win. But you did. You won the hearts of everyone who watched you. No one has ever seen someone from Kuemper fight like you fought. You're my champion, you're my brother and I love you."

I wiped tears from my eyes.

"If I were Gable I'd want you on my team," she added.

Coach Greenfield put his arm around me and walked with me toward the stands. My mother, father and brothers were there waiting.

"Matt, we love you so much," my mother said, kissing me on the cheek, squeezing me tighter than any other time in her life.

My father wrapped his arms around me from behind at the same time. Into my ear he whispered, "You're our champion, Matt. We're damn proud of you."

But their words were no relief. I hurt like Wayne Love must have hurt when he lost to me. The bruising, dagger-like agony of defeat was unwelcome company in my heart.

Time and a change of heart would be the only cure for my pain, the only thing that could seal the wound in my soul. Words could not penetrate the armor of angst I felt. Even the kindest, most thoughtful words, from those who loved me the most.

During the awards presentation for the 167-pound class, I stood on the victory stand, one step from the top. Two points away.

I could've smiled when 15,000 people clapped as my name was introduced and a silver medal was hung around my neck. I could've smiled knowing I was on television at that moment, before the entire state of Iowa. I could have, alright.

But after you give it everything you have, after you lose by a close margin when you wanted to win so badly – you don't want to stand before a mass of people, showing the pain on your face. It would be far easier to stay in the locker room, where I could privately release my frustration, sadness and disappointment.

But I would not sulk in private. I would face the truth. I would do as Dan Gable did when he lost his final collegiate match. I would follow his example. I would follow the words he once wrote for all wrestlers to see:

"There is no mat space for malcontents or dissenters. One must neither celebrate insanely when he wins nor sulk when he loses. He accepts victory professionally, humbly; he hates defeat, but makes no poor display of it."

I bit my bottom lip to hold back the tears when the cameras clicked and the spotlight showed the reality of what transpired. I accepted my place on the ladder of achievement as the television cameras scanned the faces of the six men who remained when the fighting in the 167-pound class ended.

Twenty-three

The pain I felt in losing reached its peak when I closed the door to Coach Greenfield's car and walked the seven steps leading to our front door. Hanging from the doorway of the porch was the poster my sister had made:

"WELCOME HOME CHAMP!"

I wanted to grab the poster and tear it to pieces, but I couldn't. I just reached up and pulled it down, then I shuffled over it while walking into our empty house. I kicked my shoes off and went to the medicine cabinet – a place otherwise known as "the freezer." Sitting inside the chilling frost was the best drug I could possibly ask for at the time: a half-gallon of Butterfinger ice cream. I finished it – all of it, and went to bed.

In the morning, when I awoke, I heard the familiar sound of my mother walking up the stairs to my bedroom.

"Matt, are you awake?" she asked, knocking on the door.

"Yeah, I'm up."

"May I come in for a moment."

"Sure."

When she entered she was carrying a piece of paper in her hands. "Matt, I wanted to give this to you," she said. "Would you like something to eat? You must be very hungry."

"No, not right now. I just want to rest awhile longer," I said while taking the paper she handed to me.

"Okay, let me know when you want something to eat. Matt, I love you. You have nothing to be ashamed of. We're all so proud of you."

She turned and walked down the stairs as I read the words typed on the paper. They were the most encouraging words she could have brought me. They gave me a new feeling of enthusiasm and confidence. I read them silently to myself, then aloud. They were called **The Five Attitudes Toward Failure**, written by Tom Hopkins. They read as follows:

> *I never see failure as failure, but only as a learning experience.*

> *I never see failure as failure, but only as the negative feedback I need to change course in my direction.*

> *I never see failure as failure, but only as an opportunity to develop my sense of humor.*

> *I never see failure as failure, but only as the game I must play to win.*

> *I never see failure as failure, but only as the opportunity to practice my techniques and perfect my performance.*

After reading this list of ways to handle failure I began to think about the many good things I had accomplished in my career instead of dwelling on my latest defeat. Humor, as well as time, had always been a good antidote for coping with my disappointments, and I could find a lot of humor in my career when I looked back far enough. Some of the events that I now saw as humorous, were not funny when they happened – but now, with space and time, I saw them with a different eye.

One such incident happened when I was in seventh grade. I had never worn a headgear before. And I didn't know how to put it on when it was time for me to compete.

Not only that, but the headgears our team had to wear were strange. The straps were made of tight elastic and the cups that fit over my ears had an unidentifiable front and back, making it impossible for me to figure out which direction the equipment should face. I put the headgear on as best I could figure and although I was getting choked by one of the straps, I continued to wrestle, and no one told me I had it on wrong.

The score was tied 2-2, when I started to feel sick to my stomach. I was holding onto my opponent's leg, trying to take him down, then, without any warning, the inside of my guts spilled out on the tights of my opponent's leg. The match was stopped. My coach came out to see what was wrong.

"I can't breathe," I said.

The coach noticed how one strap was pressing against my throat and unsnapped my headgear. "Well, no wonder," he said. "Your head gear is on backwards."

Today I recall the memory with a smile on my face. It was embarrassing at the time and it's quite possible that many people would have given the sport up if the same had happened to them. But I didn't. I stuck with the sport when it was the most difficult for me; when I didn't have good techniques; when I didn't have a winning record. Now I had credentials. I didn't win a state title but I was a winner in many other ways. No more time would be wasted in self-pity; no more agonizing daydreams over my loss. There was so much more I could still accomplish. All I needed to do was take time to continually recall and relive my successes, then set new goals and start working toward the achievement of them.

"National collegiate wrestling champion" sounded like a worthwhile goal. It was something I could achieve if I worked hard for another four years. But in order to achieve such a goal I would need to begin training immediately. So I stuffed some workout gear into a gym bag and went downstairs.

"Matt, where are you going?" my mom asked. "Aren't you going to stay around home and rest?"

"There's no time for resting. I have a new goal to fulfill, a new mountain to climb."

"You're not going to work out the day after the state tournament, Matt," she said, not believing what she was seeing. "Don't you want me to cook you something to eat?"

"Every day I rest is a wasted day. I've got work to do. I can always eat later," I said, opening the front door.

As I ran down the streets to the city's recreation center where I trained each day, I saw my hometown through different eyes for the first time. The trees and grass and sidewalks were the same but I was different. I had been tested in the arena of champions and I had survived. I still wanted to go to Iowa and wrestle for Dan Gable; the man whose signature appeared on my shoes; the man who was an Olympic Champion in 1972; the man who had coached The University of Iowa to one national championship after another; the man considered to be the greatest amateur wrestler and coach the United States had ever seen. But I didn't know if I would ever get to wrestle at Iowa. Did Gable want someone on his team who took second in the state? Most of his wrestlers were two and three-time state champions.

I wasn't even a one-time state champion. And I had 32 losses in my high school career. 32 losses!

Even so, somehow there had to be a way I could still go to Iowa and wrestle for Gable. I had to figure out how.

When I returned from the Gable wrestling camp I attended in Iowa City before my junior year, I worked out in a new pair of Iowa Wrestling gear that I bought at the camp.

People occasionally asked me if I wanted to wrestle for Iowa when they saw me wearing the gear - and I always said yes. One conversation I had with an underclassman named Mark, went as follows:

"What are you wearing Iowa Wrestling gear for? Do you think you're going to wrestle at Iowa someday?"

"Yes, I do," I answered while knocking off a set of pull-ups.

"You do?" he questioned.

"Yes, I do." I repeated.

"Just how well do you think you'll do in wrestling?"

"Really well."

"How well?"

"I'm going to win the state title."

"And after you win the state title, you think a team like Iowa is going to want you?" he asked.

"That's right," I said.

"Really?"

"YEAH... really!"

"What makes you so sure about that?"

"What makes you so sure I can't?"

"Well, uh, I'm not saying you can't. I just don't want to see you set your sights too high."

"And what makes you think they're too high?"

"I don't know. I guess I want to know what you plan to do if you don't make it."

"What do you mean?"

"I mean, what will you do if you don't win the state title? What will you do if Iowa doesn't want you, even if you do win the state title? Don't you think you should have a second plan, just in case you aren't good enough to wrestle there?"

"I don't need any second plans. I'm going to make it."

"But just to be on the safe side, don't you think you should have something to fall back on?"

"Hell no," I said, gritting my teeth to show my annoyance. "It's going to work out for me. I'll do whatever it takes to make sure I'm good enough to wrestle at Iowa. Case closed, alright? Now get the hell out of here and leave me alone."

The case was open now. What was I going to do if Iowa didn't want me? Was I really good enough to wrestle for Gable? My senior season was finished and I hadn't received a single letter from a single college. No one had shown an interest in me before the state meet. What about now?

The top six medalists in the 167-pound class - left to right, Joe Nekvinda, Jeff Roman, Matt Furey, Fritz Stratton, Wayne Love, Jim Sturdevant

Twenty-four

On Monday morning I sat at the kitchen table eating a plate of scrambled eggs. My mom and dad were there, and so was Duke. Fumes from his cigar bounced off his clothes and he was quacking loud enough to bring the bacon frying in the skillet back to life.

"Well, boy, I want you to know how proud the whole city of Carroll is of you. All the men down at the donut shops haven't stopped talking about you," he said.

"Thanks," I said.

"You know, Matt, did you get a chance to see the two boys from Coon Rapids rassle?" Duke questioned.

"I only got to see Marty Davis' match. He was losing, 13-7, but came back and won, 17-14."

"That was one helluva match, wasn't it? But did you see that Kim Reis at 185? Whoooee, that son of a gun is sharper than a machette with his technique. He thumped his guy, 13-5, in the finals. It was no contest."

"I'm sure it wasn't. Reis is one bad dude," I said.

"So tell me," Duke continued, "What was it like wrestling Wayne Love?"

"He was the toughest dude I ever wrestled in my life," I said. "He was so fast and so slick – but he couldn't maintain a hard pace with me for six minutes. He looked close to death during the last thirty seconds."

"Coach Greenfield said he was your toughest match," my dad added. "He wishes you didn't have to face him in the quarterfinals. He said beating him was like hitting your peak before the finals."

"Maybe so," I said.

"Did you see what **The Des Moines Register** says," said Duke, holding up the sports section. "It says that this is the first state wrestling tournament in 50 years in which someone from Waterloo failed to win a state title."

"Is that right?" my father said.

"Uh-huh," I mumbled.

"Did you know Matt had a dream last Tuesday about beating Love?" my mom said. "God talks to us in our dreams."

"Yep, the Almighty works in mysterious ways," said Duke.

"Matt," my father said, changing the subject, "you should make a list of all the people you need to thank for all the help they gave you during your high school career."

"No problem," I said. "I already planned on doing that."

* * * * *

When I walked through the doors at school, one person after another came up to me and congratulated me, telling me how they watched the championship match on television.

"I'll bet you start getting letters from every school in the nation," someone said.

"We'll see," I replied.

At ten o'clock that morning I sat in study hall with Steve Nurse. "Just think," he said, "you might have started a new tradition here. Maybe Kuemper will start sending people to the state finals every year."

"Maybe," I said.

I took out a few sheets of paper as we continued to talk, and started to make note of the people I wanted to thank. Pretending to myself that I would be giving a speech about my experiences at the state meet, I wrote an introduction and a conclusion along with a list of people I wanted to thank, then I included a few phrases of inspiration to pass on. At the time I wrote all this down I didn't know there would be a pep assembly called later that afternoon to honor me for my achievement, and that I would be asked to speak. The words I had written were mainly my method of keeping myself motivated to continue on the path of mastery.

When I finished writing I folded the papers and stuck them inside my pocket – with no idea that, in a few hours, I would be reading them out loud to the entire student body.

At 2:30 in the afternoon a special assembly was called. To my surprise, many of my classmates' parents were at the assembly as well as my mom and dad, who sat next to me in the front row. The auditorium was excitedly silent when Fr. Geelan walked to the podium, grabbed the microphone and said, "Today we are taking time to recognize and honor Matt Furey, who so beautifully represented Kuemper High School in the Iowa State High School Wrestling Championships this past weekend in Des Moines."

As I sat listening to the opening I thought about what was happening before me. I thought about all the times I had imagined giving a speech about success to the entire school. I thought about the times I had imagined them clapping and applauding me for the words I would speak. But never, never ever did I think this day would become a reality. Those thoughts were mere daydreams; ruminations.

Dreams kept my mind filled with enthusiasm and gusto, they gave me inspiration to endure the rigorous training regimen I put myself through each day. Until that moment in time, I never realized how strongly the images you focus on influence your destiny; I didn't realize that these thoughts, in some strange way, help map out and create the life you desire for yourself.

When Fr. Geelan completed his opening statement, the restrained silence in the auditorium erupted into unbridled applause. Everyone was clapping and yelling and screaming. They were standing on their feet, whistling through their teeth and loudly chanting, "FUREY, FUREY, FUREY."

I remained calm through all of it. I would be humble; at least I would try. The praise… I acted as if I had received it one thousand times before. All the putdowns, and all the boos I heard in assemblies from upper classmen in previous years, were behind me now.

"We would now like to welcome the mayor of the city of Carroll to the microphone," Fr. Geelan continued.

The mayor walked to the podium, paused until the students were silent then said, "On behalf of the city of Carroll, I congratulate Matt Furey. He has made all of us extremely proud to know him and we wish him the best in the future. Thank you, Matt Furey. You're a champion to all of us."

1,100 students and teachers stood and clapped for almost a minute.

"We would now like Matt Furey to come forward so we can re-present him with the medal he won this past weekend," Fr. Geelan said, taking the microphone in hand again.

I stood up, wiped my palms against my brown corduroy pants, and slowly, deliberately walked to the center of the floor. Fr. Geelan placed the silver medal around my neck and shook my hand. The crowd jumped to their feet again. A smile spread across my face. A smile as wide as a wrestling room – a place I thought of as home.

"Would you like to say a few words?" Fr. Geelan whispered to me as the crowd chanted, "SPEECH, SPEECH, SPEECH."

"I would like that very much," I said.

He waved me toward the microphone with his right hand. I pulled the folded speech from my pants, flattened it on the podium, cleared my throat, paused for a moment, looked into the eyes of the crowd and began:

Wrestling in the state tournament this past weekend was an extremely gratifying experience for me. I went there with plans to win the title and I came up a bit short. It was painful to come so close to victory, but I have learned a lot from this loss, and as of now, I am beginning to see it as a blessing. Instead of seeing my loss as a failure, I see it as a learning experience, and I plan on having a lot more successful experiences in the future.

Many of you have been exceptionally kind to me today, congratulating me on what I did accomplish, and I am thankful for this and want you to know how much I appreciate it.

There are always many people involved in any significant endeavor, people who help make dreams become a reality. At this time I would like to thank all those who have contributed to my career:

First of all, I'd like to thank my parents for supporting me, for going to all my matches, for consoling me in defeat and for praising me after victory.

I'd like to thank Coach Greenfield for the great job he has done in training me. He has been my coach for four years and I will miss hearing his voice when I leave town and attend college next fall.

I'd like to thank Coach Kane, who started me on the wrestling path when I was a freshman and has continued to help me throughout each season of my career.

I'd like to thank my brother Tim for helping me during my morning and evening workouts. He was a great partner. He patiently let me drill the moves

I needed to perfect on him over and over. Sometimes I would do the same move on him a hundred times in a row and he never complained once. Thank you, Tim.

I'd also like to thank my sister Sheila and brother Mal for coming to the state meet to cheer for me. It meant a lot to me.

I'd also like to thank all the others who went to the state tournament and cheered for me, and I thank all the people who watched the match on television.

I'd like to thank my friend, Duke, for his encouragement and support and for helping me get treatment for my ankle when it was injured before the district tournament.

I'd like to thank Dan Mack, from the physical therapy unit of St. Anthony's hospital, for getting my sprained ankle in shape. Without his help I wouldn't have made it to the district tournament much less the state tournament.

I'd like to thank my workout partners, Russ Hoffman, Joe Clark and Tom Feldman, for helping me acquire the physical and mental strength to accomplish my goals.

I'd like to thank my brothers for beating the heck out of me when I was younger. Without getting whooped so often by them, I don't know if I would have done so well.

Above all else, I'd like to thank God for giving me the desire, the courage and the guts to become a better wrestler.

I'd like to conclude by telling you the most valuable lesson I've learned in my life. Before going to the state tournament this past weekend, the only thing I cared about was winning. I wanted to win the state title more than anything I've ever done in my life. I wanted to win it in order to receive the respect and admiration of all of you.

Losing in the finals made me feel like I had completely failed. After my loss, I saw only tragedy. I refused to see any possible benefit arising out of my loss. To me failure was FAILURE. There was no blessing in it.

When I woke up yesterday, my mother brought me some motivating words and after I read them an inspiring thought came to me that helped wipe away the self-pity and frustration I was feeling. I'd like to share this thought with you. It goes like this:

"A man is never beaten so long as he keeps getting back up for one more round. Any man who keeps getting up after every knockdown,

every defeat, every set-back and every failure… is unbeatable. He is the unbeatable man."

Well, I'm back on my feet again. I'm up for another round.

Thank you."

ROAR.

The crowd stood up one more time, giving me an ovation that still echoes in my mind today. It's salve to my soul whenever my dreams remind me of those final five seconds.

Matt Furey,
age 17.
Senior season.

Twenty-five

The Kuemper Future Wrestler's tournament began the following Monday. Young boys' eyes glowed with excitement and intrigue as they watched me demonstrate the moves that carried me to the state finals. While they were laying the foundation for their future high school careers – mine was finished. It wasn't that long ago that I was in their position, so I coached them with the idea that one day, at least one of them would surpass my accomplishments.

We trained the kids for two hours that day – then the newspaper crew came to take pictures of the group. I looked at the happy faces posing for the camera and thought about the scrapbooks I had at home that contained the photos from each year I attended the clinic. It didn't seem possible that I was once the same size as the kids being photographed.

When I was stripping off my gear before heading home, Dennis O'Grady entered the locker room with his spiral-bound notebook in hand. He was preparing his next story for the local paper, and upon seeing me, he stopped.

"Hey, Furey, so glad to see you. I have something to tell you," he said.

"What is it?" I asked.

"I ate breakfast with Gable and some other coaches from Iowa this morning in Waterloo. They're getting ready to come to Carroll for an I-Club banquet to raise funds for the university's athletic department."

"Really?" I said, anticipating another chance to meet my idol.

"Yeah, really. And Gable said he wants you on his team. He saw you wrestle at the state meet. He saw you beat Wayne Love."

"He did?"

"He did, honest. He told me that he was there to watch Love because he wanted to recruit him to wrestle at Iowa. But when he saw you beat him he asked his assistant, 'Who's this guy from Carroll Kuemper? I never heard of anyone wrestling in the state meet from there.'"

"No kidding?" I said, as goose bumps plastered my skin.

"It's true. And when he found out you were the only one on the team at the state meet, he figured you had to have a lot of untapped potential to get as far as you did. He knows you couldn't have had very good workout partners to train with. He figures if you go to Iowa, where you'll have a whole room of champions to train with, you can really develop."

Was O'Grady telling me the truth or blowing smoke? I found out for sure a few days later when the principal delivered an envelope to me, while I was in class.

In the return address on the envelope it said, **IOWA WRESTLING**. I opened the letter and read the following,

> ### Dear Matt,
>
> *Congratulations on your recent victories at the state championships in Des Moines. We were impressed with your talent and would like to invite you to come to The University of Iowa for a recruiting trip some time within the next month.*
>
> *We will be calling you in a few days to arrange a time for your visit.*
>
> *Sincerely,*
>
> ### Chuck Yagla
> *Assistant Wrestling Coach*
> *University of Iowa*

Twenty-six

In the middle of August, six months after taking second in the state, I walked outside my house, looked at the water tower hovering above me and began packing our family car with the gear that would sustain me. I was headed to the University of Iowa where I would wrestle for Dan Gable and the Iowa Hawkeyes.

After going to Iowa City for a recruiting trip during the month of April, I was sold on the dream I envisioned throughout my high school career. And so, when letters poured in from other colleges and universities from around the country, I ignored them. As far as I was concerned, there was only one choice for me. It was one I'd made long ago.

I wanted to go where the champions trained. The state champions, the national champions, the world and Olympic champions.

Unlike almost everyone else on the Iowa squad, I was not a blue-chip recruit. I was just a regular guy who was happy to be able to say he was going to share mat space with the best there ever was. I was also the type of person who would continue to give everything he had in pursuit of his new goal: winning a national title.

Even though I wasn't even a one-time state champion, Gable and the other Iowa coaches didn't look down on me. They believed I had the potential to overcome the odds.

When I visited the team in Iowa City the coaches told me they would work with me anytime I wanted help. They told me they would work with me once a day, twice a day – even three times a day – if I wanted the help and asked for it. And they could point to wrestlers on the team, like Eddie Banach, who had just won his second-straight NCAA title, as proof that the Gable work-ethic molded champions.

"You see Eddie over there," said J Robinson, an Iowa assistant at the time. "He used to be the worst guy in the practice room. He used to leave practice crying. He used to get beat by the lightest guys in the room. And now look at him. He's a two-time national champion. He never quit. He never gave up. He's an example of what you can accomplish, too, if you stick with it. You've gotta be like a horse with blinders on.

Robinson compared the coaches at Iowa to the parents who see their baby fall over and over but never stop believing that their baby will eventually walk. "We're the same way," said Robinson. "We never stop believing that you can win it all. But you've got to keep getting up after each fall in order for us to help you make that happen."

Robinson's words still echo in my mind today. So do Gable's and so do the words of the other coaches and athletes I trained with in my new home; a wrestling room with black and gold mats, with ropes for climbing, bags for punching, dummies for throwing and weights for lifting.

On the walls outside the wrestling office were framed photos of the champions who had walked onto these mats before me. I thought about these men, some of whom I would be sharing mat space with upon my arrival, and the obstacles they had to overcome on the way to greatness. I thought about how one day I would love to have a framed photo resting upon those hallowed walls that said: Matt Furey – National Champion.

It was a three-and-a-half hour trip from the house I grew up in to my new home in Iowa City. The ride past the acres of tall corn stalks and miles of bean fields gave me plenty of time to think about what I wanted to accomplish and how much time and energy I was willing to devote to the pursuit of greatness. It also gave me time to think about the people in my community who scoffed at the idea of my chances of wrestling for Iowa and for Gable.

"Let me tell you something," one sports fan told my friend, Steve, who in turn, told me. "Furey will NEVER wrestle one second of one match for Iowa. Not one. Mark my words. He is in way over his head. He won't last a month in that room. He's going to get eaten alive."

This sports fan was not alone with this belief. Many others in my hometown felt the same way – and said so. Just not to me.

Oh how I wanted, how I so desperately wanted to prove these people wrong. I would use their comments as fuel to propel me toward my dreams. I would eat their criticism for breakfast and overcome it while I trained. And when I washed the salty sweat from my skin after practice, I would picture seeing these people again one day. I looked forward to the day I could look them in the eyes and say, "Hey, I have good news to report. I did MORE than wrestle one second of one match for Iowa. I won a national title."

These are the memories leading to my days as a collegiate wrestler. Let me tell you about them.

Let me tell you ALL about them…

Acknowledgements and Praise

A big thank you to Mom and Dad. You went to all my matches and supported me through trials and tribulations, victories and failures, wins and losses. I love you and will never forget all you did for me.

To my wife, Zhannie, and my children, Frank and Faith – thanks for being with me on this journey. I love you big time.

To my brothers, Sean, Kevin, Mal and Brian – all of you played an important role in helping me become a champion. To my sister, Sheila, big thanks for all your support in this project and for protecting me from harm on more than one occasion. To my brother, Tim, for helping me turn the corner in my high school career. Love you all.

To my coaches – Mr. Donnelly at the Future Kuemper Wrestler's tournament, Loren Greenfield and Bill Kane – you helped set the stage in my career and I'll never forget you.

To Marilyn Greenfield – for all the conversations in the library at school.

To Dan Gable, J Robinson, Lanny Davidson, Chuck Yagla, Mark Johnson, Mike DeAnna, Bruce Baumgartner and all the other high school and college coaches, wrestlers and trainers who helped me over the years.

To Vincent Lai, thanks for the layout and creative work.

To Eddie Baran, thanks for the friendship and superior website work.

To Caroll Brown, 1,000 thank you's for all you do.

To Mike Chapman, for your untiring devotion to the sport.

To Bernie Stroh for supporting this book long before it went to press.

To Mike Narey at Quality Mat Company in Waterloo, thanks for the great mats.

To Dan & Patricia Cardona, thanks for the excellent feedback on this project.

To Fan Hua Ming and Zhang Yan, thanks for the time with family each summer.

And to anyone else mentioned in this book, thanks for being part of my life.

About the Author

Matt Furey was a member of three NCAA championship teams (1982-84) for the University of Iowa, where he was coached by the legendary Dan Gable, a 1972 Olympic Gold Medalist. In 1985, Furey won an NCAA II wrestling title at 167-pounds for Edinboro University of Pennsylvania, where he trained under the guidance of 2x Olympic Gold Medalist, Bruce Baumgartner and Mike DeAnna – a 4x All-American.

After college Furey delved into the study of martial arts. In 1997, he went to Beijing, China, where he won a world title in shuaijiao kung fu, becoming the first foreigner to ever win the title in China. Upon his return to the U.S., Furey began to spread his knowledge about successful living through his many books, courses and seminars. He is the author of the world-wide best-seller, **Combat Conditioning** and many other courses, available at **MattFurey.com**

Today, Furey's seminars and coaching programs for business, fitness and personal development are sold-out events. Along with his wife and two children, they live in Tampa, Florida, and Hainan Island, China.

Matt Furey

is available for seminars, keynotes,
coaching and consulting in
business and personal development.

Direct all inquiries to:

Matt Furey
c/o Gold Medal Publications, Inc.
10339 Birdwatch Drive
Tampa, Florida 33647

email: matt@mattfurey.com
FAX: (813) 994-4947

Combat Conditioning
– the Cartoon Edition

If you wondered how Matt got into such phenomenal shape, it's simple... **Combat Conditioning**. Now you can get into the same great shape he's in and follow the same exercise regimine Matt does with your own copy of **Combat Conditioning**. With 48 super effective bodyweight exercises along with seven different programs that will get you into kick-butt shape fast. Your total investment in this no-nonsense offer is only $39.95 (plus S&H). Ordering is easy. Simply fill out the form below and fax/mail it or visit **www.mattfurey.com** to order it online.

Fill in the form below and FAX to 813 994 4947.

Or send by mail to:
Gold Medal Publications, Inc.
10339 Birdwatch Drive
Tampa, FL 33657

Name: _____

Address: _____

City: _____ State/Province: _____

Zip/Postal Code: _____

Phone: _____ FAX: _____

Email: _____

Website: _____